★★★

WHITE COLLAR

WARRIOR

LESSONS FOR SALES PROFESSIONALS
FROM AMERICA'S MILITARY ELITE

COACH BILL HART
WITH BILL BLANKSCHAEN

PostHill
PRESS

A POST HILL PRESS BOOK

ISBN: 978-1-68261-528-7
ISBN (eBook): 978-1-68261-529-4

White Collar Warrior:
Lessons for Sales Professionals from America's Military Elite
© 2018 by Coach Bill Hart with Bill Blankschaen
All Rights Reserved

Cover art by Cody Corcoran

Post Hill Press
New York • Nashville
posthillpress.com

Published in the United States of America

DEDICATION

This book is dedicated to the men and women who stepped up to serve this country in uniform. Your dedication, commitment, and patriotism inspire me.

Petty Officer Second Class (SEAL) Michael A. Monsoor, your selfless bravery and extreme valor remind me to dig deeper every day and be the best I can be because of your ultimate sacrifice.

For my love, Toni. Without your encouragement and support, this book would not exist. Thank you for all that you bring to my life. Your eyes are the first thing I look forward to seeing in the morning, and the last thing that I see at night. I love you.

CONTENTS

WHAT IT MEANS TO BE
A WHITE COLLAR WARRIOR

Elite warriors know a secret—if you want to be the best, you have to learn from the best and give them permission to push you far beyond your comfort zone.

In *White Collar Warrior*, author and Coach Bill Hart shares what he's learned from interviewing military elite warriors, discovering how they respond to training, discipline, fear, planning, failure, motivation, and teams. He found that there are strong similarities between the practices of the military elite and the practices of elite sales professionals.

Drawing on his years of coaching high-performing sales leaders, Hart will walk you through the process you need to take to become a different kind of warrior—a White Collar Warrior. Paying respects to the servicepeople who have worn the uniform, Hart offers a no-nonsense guide to getting things done. If you want to take your sales performance to the next level, this book is a field manual for making it happen. It is jam-packed with insights and tools that will help you stop talking and start doing.

Success begins in the mind, and *White Collar Warrior* will help you conquer fear, capture potential, and become a sales warrior.

AUTHOR'S NOTE

While every attempt has been made to honor the special military community of the Special Forces—the best of the best the United States military produces—there may be errors in abbreviations, references, or vernacular. If so, I apologize as a civilian doing his best to understand this unique culture. To every veteran who has ever served our country in uniform, whether you served in combat or not (an important distinction, I've learned from many of you), I thank you from the bottom of my heart for being willing to step into the gap.

FOREWORD

When I think of our military men and women, the words sacrifice, honor, duty, and responsibility come to mind. My dad served in the United States Navy at the end of World War II. As a veteran, Dad took special care to thank our troops whenever the opportunity presented itself. It was common for us, as we traveled across the country, to spend a few minutes with our uniformed warriors, expressing our gratitude for them, just barely boarding an airplane before the doors were closed. Dad realized the sacrifice each person was making and the high standard of honor, duty, and responsibility to which they were committed.

White Collar Warrior: Lessons for Sales Professionals from America's Military Elite is a book that perfectly illustrates the high calling sales professionals have, and how to live up to that calling. One of the characteristics of the military elite is simple, yet profound—they choose to do the work, to train, and to keep going, even when the mind and body want to give up. In a different way, sales professionals have exactly the same choices to make—to do the work, to train, and to keep going, even though the rejections are building up and the results are delayed again and again.

I am grateful you are picking up this book and reading it. The techniques and skills Coach Bill Hart has laid out for you will most certainly improve your results as a sales professional. However, there is a bigger reason I am grateful. In my dad's classic book, *Secrets of Closing the Sale*, he gives hundreds of examples of how to close the sale— but none of these *hows* were as important as the *why*. Bill made sure this book, like Dad's classic, is built on the *why*, because when you truly know your *why*, you can persevere through the tough times.

As an elite sales professional, just like an elite military warrior, you are held to a higher standard. Your training will give you incredible skills. How will you use them? I learned an important lesson from one of my mentors, Rabbi Daniel Lapin. He taught me that in the Hebrew language, there are several words for helping someone. One of those words has a high moral meaning and is also the word used to describe the profession of sales. In this view, to sell means to look into the future of your prospects and anticipate a problem or challenge they will likely encounter, and then offer them a solution before they ever experience the pain of that problem. Now that is a high moral calling!

Elite military professionals and elite sales professionals understand that the better they prepare today, the more capable they will be of preventing those they love from experiencing pain in the future. Yes, love of country and love of people are ultimately what makes the elite, elite. This book is a dynamic tool that will help you create the future you want for yourself, because it will show you how to help other people get the future they want. People are counting on you. Get started now!

—Tom Ziglar
CEO of Ziglar
Key collaborator on *Born to Win*

CHAPTER 1

A TALE OF
TWO WARRIORS

The sun is still a rumor in Coronado, California, when the deafening staccato of gunfire rips Rick from his bunk and launches him to his feet. Blinding flashes punch through the dark outside the barracks window, creating a strobe effect that makes the scrambling men within appear to move in slow motion. Suddenly, Rick hears the door kicked open, and yells fill the room. As he staggers toward the noise, he sees a shadowy figure fill the frame and hears a voice thick with authority growl: "Welcome to hell, gentlemen."

Talk about a wake-up call! This is Hell Week—every Navy SEAL candidate can't wait for it to start and prays he'll survive to see it end. It's the week in the midst of BUD/S (Basic Underwater Demolition SEAL) training that will determine whether Rick has what it takes to be the best of the best, the elite of the military world. Hell Week is the defining event of BUD/S training. It is held early on—in the third week of First Phase—before the Navy makes an expensive investment in SEAL operational training. Hell Week consists of five and a half days of cold, wet, brutally difficult operational training.

From this first rude awakening, Rick will likely not sleep more than four hours for the next five and a half days. Icy surf will pummel him to the brink of hypothermia. Gritty sand will rub his skin raw as he moves from sea to land and runs for mile after unending mile. Sleep deprivation will cause every candidate to question the decision to attempt this. Countless push-ups, sit-ups, and excruciating flutter kicks will inflame every muscle in his entire body. All of it will introduce him to himself, to discover what even he may not yet know—does he have what it takes to become the best? Rick will discover what the veteran instructors already know—if he even entertains the thought of quitting, he's not going to survive the week.

As he moves toward the pulsating light and sound of gunfire outside, Rick knows most of the candidates alongside him will set their helmet down, "ring the bell," and be gone before they're done. With teeth clenched, he has time for just one thought before being swept out into the chaos: "They will *not* make me quit!"

The Definition of Elite in the Military World

The challenge our imaginary candidate, Rick, faces stems from the desire to become the best at something. Maybe you can relate to it. What child hasn't imagined scenarios in which he or she becomes the best in the world? You can fill in the blank with your own childhood aspirations, but for those who aspire to be members of the US military, the ultimate dream is often to serve among the best, the elite of the US military who serve in the groups collectively known as Special Operations Forces (SOF). They are the warriors who achieve what most only imagine. They are the ones who get the call when all other options have failed and whose accomplishments, when they do their job well, we often never know. And they have much to teach us if we are willing to learn.

It may surprise you to learn how many Special Forces groups there are and yet how few people qualify to join their ranks. Most of us are familiar with the Navy SEALS (the name refers to their versatility in operating by Sea, Air, and Land) or the Army Rangers. When I was a kid, I thought the Army Green Berets were some of the coolest guys in uniform. And yet there are numerous groups that function as SOF across all military branches, including Marine Corps MARSOC Raider, and Air Force Special Operations teams.

Other elite groups exist alongside these Special Operations Forces, of course, but these groups form the core of US Special Operations Forces. Many people try to enter, to become one of the best, but few succeed.

Now don't get me wrong, all of our servicepeople are heroes, deserving of our highest respect and thanks. That's especially true when you consider that for nearly two generations, no American has been obligated to join, and few do. Less than .5 percent of the population serves in the armed forces, compared with more than 12 percent during World War II. When you look at the numbers above in that light, you see that these people represent 1 percent of just .5 percent of the entire US population. Clearly there are many highly qualified people, in a variety of disciplines who didn't volunteer to serve in the military, of course, but when we talk about the very best in the US military, we're clearly talking about some pretty rarified air.

They endure a grueling process to gain that status of *elite warrior*. My friend, Chad Fleming, a former Army Ranger, gives just a glimpse into the training process that reveals the identities of these warriors, often surprising even themselves:

[The] physical training is tough and taxing on the mind and body. You learn more about yourself and your own breaking point than anything else. During physical training, you learn about how different people are affected when you throw stress at them. It took me two times to get through Ranger School. The first time, I had a full-blown heatstroke doing the Ruck March. It's a fast march of fifteen to twenty-two miles over rugged terrain with fifty to sixty pounds on your back. I was running on a little more than three hours of sleep.

After I got healed up, they wouldn't let me go back until winter class. When it was time for the Ruck March again, I was mentally dreading it. I thought, What if it happens again? At the twelve- to twelve-and-a-half-mile mark, I had to really dig down deep. In Ranger School, you have a Ranger buddy, and mine said, "I can tell you're sucking. You cannot let this get you."

He wanted to take some of my gear. I'm a type-A guy and decided, "No, you're not taking my gear. I got it." It wasn't about letting myself down; it was about not letting the other down—the person to the left and right.

Chad survived the march—and the rest of Ranger School. But only half of all who apply to Ranger School make the cut, and that attrition rate is even higher for other SOF groups! Air Force Special Operations has an attrition rate of 60 percent; the Army Green Berets, 70 percent; and the Navy Seals, 80 percent! That means that 80 percent of the most physically fit and well-conditioned people in the nation quit and go home. If our imaginary SEAL trainee Rick survives the process, he'll watch just about everybody who started alongside him turn back before it's over. In short, those who succeed as elite warriors have gone through hell and then some to become the best of the best.

But are they the only ones who must endure a challenging process to become the elite? Certainly, few people will ever face the physical demands placed on them. But as a coach to high-performing sales professionals and leaders, I have spent a few decades getting to know another group of high-caliber people who have quite a bit in common with them in spite of their seemingly disparate circumstances. Allow me to introduce you to the elite from a different world, one with which you may be more familiar: the world of the sales professional extraordinaire.

A Different Kind of Warrior

Halfway across the country, in a sleepy suburb of St. Louis, Missouri, the blaring alarm sounds, slapping Scott from his slumber. The moon is still high in the sky, streaming boldly through his bedroom window as if unconcerned that the sun will arrive in a few hours to replace it. Scott opens one bleary eye to see the same number that greets him every morning, staring back at him, red and unblinking—4:00 a.m.

For a brief moment, he fights the urge to tap the alarm back into silence and burrow under the covers for another hour of sleep. Finally, his legs swing over the edge of the bed as if pushed out from under the covers by force of habit. As he stands, he silences the insistent beeping and slips his smartphone from its charger. He staggers toward the coffee pot and pours himself a cup. He sips the hot java as he slips into his usual chair.

Scott pauses briefly to savor the silence before reaching for his well-worn life and business plans—a regular review that calibrates his every morning. After reconnecting with his mission, he opens an app and reviews his priorities for the day, highlighting those that will test his mettle most but yield the greatest return. Today will decide whether Scott has what it takes to continue to be the best of the best, the elite of the sales world. He is a warrior of a different sort than Rick—a sales professional who knows that if he even entertains the thought of quitting, he will fail.

He downs the last of his coffee and notes that his morning calendar shows an intense physical workout, followed by breakfast with his children and a quick check-in with his support team before a day full of back-to-back meetings with potential clients. He breathes deeply and opens his laptop to review emails, his mind already rehearsing the script he performs with precision each day: "Do what most will not do, to enjoy what most never will."

Two Worlds, One Warrior

To be among the elite in the sales world does not necessarily mean you have to wake up at 4:00 a.m. like our imaginary sales friend Scott. But it might. His commitment and drive are typical of what I have observed at the highest levels of sales success. To be the best means you do what few others will to achieve what most others only imagine—and you do it each and every day.

At first glance, Rick, a Navy SEAL candidate at the Naval Special Warfare Training Center, and Scott, a thirtysomething national sales leader from the suburbs, might not appear to have much in common. But what these two professionals share is a daily battle to be the very best at what they do. One faces physical and mental challenges defending freedom in sacrificial service for his country, service that cannot be praised highly enough; the other wages a meaningful war of a different sort that significantly impacts his dreams, family, company, and community.

For nearly two decades, I've had the privilege of coaching sales professionals and leaders to be the very best they can be. I've interviewed hundreds of the sales elite to discover what makes them great. I'd always had a deep respect for the US military, but when I read the book *Lone Survivor* a few years ago, I was deeply moved by Navy SEAL Marcus Luttrell's account of his experience in Afghanistan. I was so moved, in fact, that I started to do something about it.

I encountered a grassroots initiative called Boot Campaign based in Texas (www.bootcampaign.org). Started in 2009 by five women from Texas known as the Original Boot Girls, the Boot Campaign proudly provides life-improving programs for veterans and military families nationwide to bridge the divide between military life and civilian life. Boot Campaign encourages all Americans to "lace up" and "get their boots on" as an easy and tangible way to express patriotism and gratitude for all who serve. The goal of the campaign is to see all Americans put on combat boots to raise awareness of the needs of our more than 21 million veterans and to thank the more than 1.2 million active duty military serving in 150 countries globally and stateside.

I eventually had the privilege of emceeing some of the group's events and connecting with former members of the military, including those engaged in various branches of our military's Special Operations. I started asking questions, applying my years of interviewing experience to these former members of the elite military forces, who very graciously and patiently responded. What I heard lifted my admiration for them to an even higher place. These were patriots of the highest caliber who gave more than most of us could ever imagine giving to achieve their objective.

But then a light went on. As I listened to discover more about the world of the military elite, I started to see connections, critical lessons common to the elite of both worlds—military and sales. Again and again, I saw that the steps needed to be the best—and stay there—were the same. Most important, I realized that it's more than just natural talent that separates the best from the rest. Sure, talent is a definite advantage, but the lessons I was gleaning from conversations with veterans of elite groups like the Navy SEALs and Army Rangers were lessons that *could* be learned. I began to see that becoming one of the elite is largely a decision you make, not once but every day. It is indeed something that you become. And when we support the lessons with structured practices and proven methods—look out!

I believe that by following these lessons from the US military elite, any sales professional, man or woman, can become a White Collar Warrior who fills his or her lungs each and every day with rarified air, the breath of the elite. And by "any sales professional," I mean *you*.

Let's be clear about one thing: the elite of the military world make tremendous sacrifices. Their devotion to defending our freedom and one another deserves a special recognition. They are heroes. The families who support them and endure extended absences as they serve are heroic families. And for those who pay the highest price in service to our nation, we can offer nothing but eternal respect, honor, and gratitude. If we spent the entire book praising these warriors, we would still fall short of honoring them sufficiently. There is no shortage of moving stories of their courage and sacrifice in the face of danger, but one in particular moves me like few others.

Michael "Mikey" Monsoor became one of the elite when he received his Navy SEAL trident in 2004 and headed to Iraq as part of Delta platoon in April 2006. He had just turned twenty-five. He trained Iraqi soldiers for the next five months, often engaging in combat with enemy insurgents. On September 26, 2006, a hand grenade bounced off his chest pack and landed on the rooftop where he and his SEAL brothers were positioned. Positioned with the only opportunity to escape, Mikey instead made a split-second decision that saved the life of every other man on that roof. He dove onto the grenade, smothering the blast with his own body. He died shortly afterward from his wounds. Two of the three SEAL snipers were injured; however, there were no other fatalities. In 2008, President George W. Bush presented Mikey's parents with the Medal of Honor, the highest US military tribute, for the heroic sacrifice.

When I think about Michael Monsoor's bravery and the selfless character that would cause him to take such action without hesitation, I'm struck speechless and moved deeply. To remind myself of this perspective, this unimaginable commitment to one's fellow warriors, I wear his KIA (Killed in Action) bracelet every day and frequently close my talks with his story. One of the final things Mikey said was "No Regrets." What a powerful mantra. I don't know about you, but I want to learn what moves someone to such heroism. How did he get to a place where he could so matter-of-factly do what few could even imagine doing?

Such sacrifices make it difficult to fully fathom the inner workings of such people. But the fact that they perform at such a high level in so many areas doesn't mean the principles and lessons they live by can't be transferred to your daily world of email inboxes, color-coded spreadsheets, and hurried meetings over lattes in crowded coffee shops with trendy music. No doubt your challenges look and feel different than the ones they face each day—thanks largely to their ongoing sacrifices. But the process of breaking through barriers to achieve what seems an unreachable goal is the same. You may not face a bullet when visiting a potential client, but the fear of rejection can shoot you down before you ever step inside someone's office. You may not parachute into darkness so deep you can feel it, but you sure feel the anxiety when you risk the unknown to explore a new initiative or direction in your business. You may not inch your way across a rocky surface for days toward a solitary sniper position, but when you are the first to arrive on Monday and the last to leave on Friday, your mission to be the best can feel pretty lonely.

The sacrifices are not the same, but the lessons that guide the military's elite can be transferred to the sales world and take you where you want to go. One of the elite in the sales world is Max Leaman. He's risen quickly to become one of the best in the mortgage industry. To achieve his level of success, he's had to break through barriers. Here's how he described it to me:

> *It all comes back to winning. It's all about the goal to win. Whether that means closing X number of units, having X numbers of volume, having this much money in the bank, or whatever it is, you don't quit until you get your goal. And you'll have setbacks and failures along the way, but you don't let that stop you.*
>
> *Lazy people don't persevere. Lazy people take the easy way out. Despite what my wife says about housework, I'm not lazy. I won't quit. I refuse to fail. I expect excellence from me and from my team on every deal. And to that extent, I always say to everybody, "I'm in here with my team." I work just as hard as I expect them to work, if not harder. I lead from the front. And that's kind of my motto.*

Having interviewed scores of the military elite, I see that we could change a few words in Max's description and it might just as easily have come from an Army Ranger confronting battlefield obstacles. Whether he identifies it or not, Max functions each day by the lessons the military elite live by, lessons we'll unpack together in the pages ahead. And they are lessons you can learn.

You Can Do This

As I mentioned earlier, the elite military group with the highest attrition rate is the Navy SEALs—over 80 percent of people drop out. The interesting thing is that, almost without exception, no one makes them quit. It's not as if they pass the tests but the gatekeepers let only a certain number join. Sure, extreme violations can get you kicked out, but for the most part, if you make it, you make it. If you don't, you don't.

In BUD/S training, anyone can quit at any time. All someone needs to do is set down his helmet in line with the many others, ring the bell, and walk away. Across the various branches of US Special Forces, you'll find similar rituals to symbolize the power of the choice each candidate must make every moment of every day. Will someone choose to continue to pursue a dream in the face of adversity, or will he or she ring the bell and drop out? It's a decision all prospective warriors must make on their own. No one can do it for them.

Marcus Luttrell, US Navy SEAL (retired) and author of *Lone Survivor*, recounts some critical advice he received from his instructor, Chief Bob Nielsen, as he prepared for SEAL training. Nielsen said: "There's only one guy in this room who knows whether you're going to make it or fail. And that's you. Go to it, gentlemen. Always give it everything." So it is with you. You are the only one who knows whether or not you really want to be the best. It's a decision you must make every day—to do what others will not do, to take one more step at the moment you feel like collapsing. Because that's what warriors do. It's what separates the good from the best, the elite from the rest.

Steven Pressfield is an acclaimed writer of historical fiction who excels at resurrecting legends of ancient warriors. Perhaps his most popular book is *Gates of Fire*, about the Spartans and the Battle of Thermopylae, which is taught at various US military academies. In his nonfiction book *The Warrior Ethos*,

Pressfield tells this story of the Theban general who was the first to defeat the Spartans at the battle of Leuctra:

> The evening before the fight, Epaminondas called his warriors together and declared that he could guarantee victory on the morrow if his men would vow to perform one feat at the moment he commanded it. The men, of course, responded aye. "What do you wish us to do?" "When I sound the trumpet," said Epaminondas, "I want you to give me one more foot. Do you understand? Push the enemy back just one foot." The men swore they would do this.
>
> Battle came. The armies clashed and locked up, shield to shield, each side straining to overcome the other. Epaminondas watched and waited till he judged both armies had reached the extremity of exhaustion. Then he ordered the trumpet sounded. The warriors of Thebes, remembering their promise, summoned their final reserves of strength and pushed the foe back only one foot. This was enough. The Spartan line broke. A rout ensued.

It's true. The difference between the good and the best is often slim—just one more step, one more handwritten note, one more call, one more early wake up while the rest of the world sleeps. Although it's easier to find other people to blame for failing to become one of the sales elite, White Collar Warriors begin the way all warriors begin—by taking a hard look at their own commitment to excellence. Mark Divine, commander, US Navy SEALs (retired), puts it bluntly: "Bottom line: If you lack an underlying commitment to self-mastery and growth, even the best theory won't help you lead yourself or a team to success." In other words, it's up to you.

The good news is that you can do this. You can become one of the elite of the sales world. It is my privilege to guide you through this book, as I've guided others just like you through these critical lessons from the elite of the US military. Together we can maximize your natural strengths and talents—and have fun doing it! But it's your choice. Your success is your responsibility. The bad news is that not all of you will choose to take the challenge to follow what I call "The Way of the Warrior." Even though you say you want to succeed, some of you will "ring the bell" and settle for less than the best. I sincerely hope that's not you. As Chief Nielsen said, only you know whether you are going to make it or fail. I know I want you to make it. I want you to become the best sales professional or leader you can be, to achieve the success you now only dream of achieving. And I'm looking forward to hearing your story when you do succeed. I can go there *with* you, but I can't go there *for* you.

In his book *Ambition*, American essayist Joseph Epstein recounts this quotation from a French writer: "The colonel who retires on a farm in the country would have liked to become a general; but if I could examine his life, I would find some little thing that he neglected to do, that he did not want to do. I could prove to him that he did not want to become a general." What the storyteller means, of course, is that the colonel did not really want to become a general enough to do what needed to be done.

Do you? I don't know the answer. Only you do, and only time will tell. But if you sense a hunger to live life amongst the elite, to be the very best, I invite you to join me in this journey to discover and apply lessons from the US military elite that will position you to become one of the elite of the rough-and-tumble world of the modern sales professional.

Perhaps it might help to think of me as your "swim buddy." During BUD/S training, each Navy SEAL candidate is assigned a swim buddy. Here's how a SEAL describes how attached swim buddies become during training:

> You work with your buddy as a team. You never separate, not even to go to the john. In IBS (that stands for "inflatable boat, small") training, if one of you falls over the side into the freezing ocean, the other joins him—immediately. Later on, in the BUD/S course proper, you can be failed out of hand, thrown out, for not staying close enough to your swim buddy.

Now I'm not necessarily suggesting you take this book with you *everywhere*—after all, we've only just met. And I don't think this book floats all that well, so you might want to avoid headfirst dives into the water. But if it helps to think of me as your swim buddy in this journey toward excellence, I'm good with that. And we'll be joined along the way by some of the elite of the sales world through exclusive interviews and input. They'll help us take the lessons we uncover and interpret them through a sales lens.

I believe you can do this; you can become one of the elite. It might require joining Scott for that 4:00 a.m. wake-up call for a daily life-plan review. But as Mark Divine puts it,

"When extraordinary efforts become commonplace, extraordinary results follow." Together we can close the gap between where you are now and where you want to be. And we'll do it one lesson at a time.

Closing the Gap

What does being the best mean to you?

- For US military elite candidates enduring grueling training sessions, the goal is clear: survive. But your goals may be more difficult to identify and different than anyone else's. Take a moment now to record the specific goals that would qualify you to belong amongst the elite.
- For example, would you define success in terms of units sold, revenue produced, or client referrals? Or would it mean receiving a specific award or attaining a certain level of sales—number one in the division, region, or even the nation? If you struggle to dream that big for now, start by defining goals that would be a significant stretch for you personally.
- Whatever it may be for you to become the best, write it down now in as concrete detail as possible. Don't focus for now on *how* you will get there, but on *where* you want to go.

_____

_____

_____

_____

_____

Do you really want to be the best?

- One thing the military elite learn quickly is that only _you_ can want to be the best. No one can force excellence upon you. If you don't have the desire to become the best, no one will stop you from settling for mediocrity. In fact, the origins of the word _mediocre_ come from mountain climbers who would make it halfway up the side of a cliff and then stop, thinking that accomplishment to be good enough.
- So ask yourself, is "good enough" going to be good enough for you? How badly do you want to achieve the goals you listed above? Describe what it would mean to you to succeed in achieving the goals you listed above.

_____

_____

_____

_____

_____

Why do you want to be the best?

- Your motivation to succeed is unique to you. It may be as simple as making money to drive a fast car and live in a big house, but for most of us, even the desire to make a lot of money has a deeper purpose. For example, you may want to be able to retire at an early age in order to travel the world with family. Or you may have a child in need of ongoing medical care. Perhaps you want to invest in innovative start-ups, build a real estate port-folio, or support charitable causes that make the world a better place. We'll explore more of how to tap into your motivation later, but take a moment now to list the reason or reasons you want to achieve the status of elite in your sales position.

_____

_____

_____

_____

_____

CHAPTER 2

WHAT IT TAKES TO BE THE BEST

*"You've got to get up every
morning with determination if you're going
to go to bed with satisfaction."*

—*George Lorimer*

Like most of the military elite, Andrew Paul doesn't look like a warrior when he's sporting a button-down shirt and bow tie while selling mortgages to his customers. But after talking to him for just a few minutes, you can sense the steel that runs through his spine. Andrew graduated with SEAL class 241 and was quickly deployed to Iraq. After several tours of duty, he retired from active duty and went into the mortgage business to apply the skills he learned as a member of the military elite.

But it was 2007, and the economy was spiraling downward. It was a lousy time to start a business, especially one that involved the mortgage industry. But for Andrew, there were many parallels between his role as a SEAL and his role as a sales professional. It all started with discipline. If he was going to become a success in the sales world, he knew he had to dig deep and stay disciplined to do the things he knew he needed to do. He knew this was true even if he didn't feel like doing it. Andrew said something to me that stuck, and I think it will help you too: "The difference between good and great is the great ones keep going. They may get knocked down, but they stand back up and make the next play." Now, in 2017, Andrew has become one of the sales elite.

To many salespeople, success remains a mystery. They're engaged in a flurry of activity to meet quotas, yet they wonder if they have what it takes to be the best. The elite warriors of the US military have led the way in defining success every day for the past two centuries. What is required of the military elite corresponds with what is required of the elite in the sales world.

But most people ring the bell right about now. They read a book to this point and then place a business card as a bookmark and leave it on the nightstand to collect dust, never to be opened again. I want more for you. I want you to become one of the sales elite, the best of the best. I want you to access a proven plan to become a White Collar Warrior who digs deep and refuses to ring the bell.

So here's a simple plan that might work for you. If you can't knock out this entire book in one sitting (and let's face it, few people can), commit to reading one chapter each week. Make an appointment with yourself to join me on this journey once every week. Chew on a chapter. Let it marinate. Be honest with yourself about where you are and where you want to go. Elite warriors drill for hours to make their training second nature. I don't expect hours, but if you'll commit to finishing this, I'll give you a plan to practice the lessons you learn. At the end of ninety days, you'll be well on your way to becoming one of the elite.

Special Operations members have a quiet confidence. It's why they often refer to themselves as "the silent professionals." So much so, that you generally have to pull their role and experience out of them. Again, this is part of their ethos—they don't lead with it. "Don't talk about it, do it." We would all be well-served to absorb that concept.

When I began interviewing and interacting with the military elite, one of the first things I noticed was how easily they transitioned into business. It was as if they carried the innate confidence and skill sets from battle into the business world. Many of them excel in sales or as entrepreneurs. It's no coincidence. They stay disciplined even when they don't have to. They stay in great shape. They own their thinking and actions.

In short, they take their warrior ethos into the business world. Consequently, when many of them cross over to civilian life, they crush it. They feel like they can do anything, and amazingly, they often do.

Be Unwilling to Fail

That's why the first step to becoming a White Collar Warrior is to believe you can. For the military elite, to even think about quitting means you're done. Confidence is key. With confidence comes a willingness to own your situation and recognize that your success depends on you. No excuses. Jocko Willink, a retired Navy SEAL, calls this "extreme ownership," and with his fellow SEAL Leif Babin, he wrote a book with this title. Stop making excuses and start making things happen. Own it.

From my perspective in the coach's chair, I've seen many people respond to the hard work of becoming better with something easier—excuses. I've heard just about all of them over the years. If you're like most people I've coached, you've already begun a mental list of the reasons why you're *not* currently maximizing your potential in the sales arena. These excuses immediately halt any progress you are making toward becoming the best.

See if any of these excuses sound familiar to you:

I don't have time to prospect. This excuse is a favorite of those who lack training. It's a classic sign of avoidance. Ineffective salespeople avoid the possibility of rejection by avoiding interaction with prospects. It's counterintuitive and self-sabotaging but incredibly common.

I don't want to be a "pushy" salesperson. Many people in sales believe that being aggressive is at the core of success. But think about it: as a consumer, odds are that you personally don't do business with pushy people. So why would you need to become one? You can better position yourself for success by learning techniques for building authentic relationships and providing genuine value.

I don't know how to respond to objections. This is where training really makes a difference. There are only so many objections out there. The best salespeople prepare ahead of time. They create a script based on common objections and rehearse so they can respond in the heat of the moment without much thinking.

I hate cold-calling. There are numerous ways to convert cold leads to warm leads *if* you are willing to learn and do. A little training can go a long way to get rid of this excuse for avoiding essential action.

I can't compete on price. Salespeople often think that price is the most important thing on a customer's mind. However, the fact of the matter is that, although price is important, it's rarely the key decision-making factor. For the most part, price is one of the last considerations customers make, and they generally weigh price against value. So, rather than worrying about discounting price, focus on building value for your clients.

We've all got plenty of excuses as to why we aren't the best. For one thing, becoming the best doesn't happen on the path of least resistance. It's not easy. But compare your worst sales nightmares with what the military elite endure. My hope is that you will use this book as a reminder of what is truly tough—crawling on your belly through mud under barbed wire while live ammo whistles overhead; swimming in water so cold, your instructor is actually waiting for you to become hypothermic; or becoming so sleep-deprived, you lose almost all connection to reality. When you consider what the elite of the military world endure to be the best, your preparation suddenly doesn't look all that tough, does it? Suck it up buttercup.

The Power of a Coach

No matter who you are or how much you excel in your field, a coach can help you take your game to the next level. Think about it. Superstar athletes still need coaches to help them improve their game and maximize their effectiveness. Singers and musicians hire coaches to help them overcome flaws and improve their skills. Even the military elite want and receive constant feedback and accountability to stay sharp. Coaches provide an objective view and share the desires of the ones they coach—to help them get a win.

I make my living helping businesspeople see their situations with a fresh set of eyes and offer a perspective on how to become the best versions of themselves. My hope is that this book can act as a virtual coaching session for you. I've distilled what I've learned down into The Way of the Warrior in the following chapters to help you be your best.

When I talk with people about coaching, I never try to talk them into it. But I do tell them what the benefit is and the reason that they might want to consider a coach. Coaching has three primary functions. First, an effective coach helps you get clear about what you want, personally and professionally. Most people think they're clear, but they're not. They have a vague idea, but coaching helps them get more specific to envision a better future and what that might look and feel like to you.

Second, once you're clear on what you want, personally and professionally, you can collaborate with your coach to create action plans that close the gaps between where you are and where you want to be. That's why each chapter in this book ends with a section called "Closing the Gap." For example, suppose I were coaching you and you told me you want to get healthy. I could tell you what you need to do: go run five miles a day and stop eating cheeseburgers. But you probably already know that. What a good coach does is work with you to come up with a solution.

I often begin by asking, "What do you think you need to do?" Usually there's a long, awkward pause—and that's a good thing. It means you're thinking about what you can do and starting to take ownership of your own solution. You might respond, "I feel I really need to cut back on drinking Dr Pepper." From there I might ask, "Interesting. How many

Dr Peppers do you drink a day?" "Three," you admit, "but I should cut back to one." We've now come up with a plan together. Admittedly, this is a simplistic example, but you get the idea. We would then record the action plan you gave me and begin putting it into practice. At Building Champions, the leadership coaching company I've worked at for the past fifteen years, once the action plan is created, it is always followed by the question, "By when?" Dates drive disciplines.

The third function of coaching is accountability. Without accountability, coaching becomes anecdotal conversations that make us feel good but don't move the needle. Accountability occurs when you verify what is important to you and then you give the coach permission to ask you about it regularly. When you empower a coach to hold you accountable, it's a game-changer.

I am passionate about coaching, because I've seen the effects it has had on so many lives—mine included, as all of the coaches at Building Champions are themselves coached. I feel a sense of responsibility for my clients and for you, because you've joined me on this journey to become the best of the best. I know how this book can help you. I've seen it happen. That's why I wrote it. Your growth is what fuels my passion to help you transform your sales career and life.

But you have a responsibility too. If you want to become a White Collar Warrior, you have to consider it your mission to become the best. You have to be productive, efficient, and effective in your work. You have to shift your mindset toward your customers from, "How can I close the sale and make a commission?" to, "How can I help my customers and serve them better?" As silent professionals, the military elite don't focus on themselves. They don't brag. They don't have to. They take pride in their training and discipline. They go out and do the task at hand. Their results speak for themselves.

Shift your mindset to one of service first, and you won't have to convince anyone you are the best. People will already know.

I co-lead a program at Building Champions called The Master's Coach. This is a group of the best of the best in one particular industry. In his book The Ideal Team Player, Patrick Lencioni refers to a litmus test for the right members as being humble, hungry, and smart. The top performers I know or personally coach would all fit into that box.

The Way of the Warrior

To become one of the best, you have to know what it takes to be the best. I know the troubles sales professionals face and the practical solutions to overcome them. As I've coached and interviewed business professionals and questioned members of the US military elite, I've discovered The Way of the Warrior, a proven path to becoming the best salesperson you can be.

You'll learn the Way of the Warrior in the seven lessons that comprise the next seven chapters of the book. These lessons are taken straight from the warriors I've interviewed and filtered through the lens of the sales professionals I've coached. Simply put, they work.

As we go through the rest of the book, here's what you will discover:

Lesson 1: Your Training Is the Foundation for Everything

In the military, training is literally a matter of life and death. Rigorous training, often to the point of mind-numbing boredom, is the foundation for every successful mission. Warriors practice for situations so they are ready when they occur. White Collar Warriors train because they know that they'll never be the best if they don't train and prepare like the best. Learn to train well, and you will be prepared for anything that comes your way.

Lesson 2: Your Discipline Will Determine Your Success

For many, *discipline* is a dirty word. It means sweating at the gym, not eating the last of the ice cream, or holding your tongue when you have a sarcastic reply. But for the warrior, discipline is the key to success. Knowing intel about your enemy, understanding the plan of attack, and staying on mission all come as a result of rigid discipline. White Collar Warriors are disciplined too. They know where they want to go and are willing to pay the price of discipline to get there. Success is on the line. Undisciplined living is unacceptable. An exceptional life—not an average one—is the outcome.

Lesson 3: Your Fear Must Become Your Friend

Facing fears can be crippling or empowering. It can provide freedom or paralysis. Everyone has something that causes fear. Warriors face that fear head on because they are well-trained and disciplined. They know what to do, and they use that fear as the impetus to spur them onward. The White Collar Warrior faces fears too: the fear of a missed sale, the fear of rejection, the fear of not making ends meet. These are all very real fears, but when you make fear your friend, you demolish its power over you. It becomes another tool to push you to become the best.

Lesson 4: Your Sales Plan Positions You for Mission Success

Warriors never go into battle without a battle plan. To do so could very well be suicide. A well-formed battle plan includes information on the lay of the land, the strength of the enemy, the position of any allies, and the target objective. Although the situation on the ground may be fluid and require adaptability, a battle plan is key to victory. White Collar Warriors need a sales plan for success. They don't just make calls when they feel like it to whoever is top of mind. They attack with a relentless energy that is dictated by the plan. The plan breaks big objectives into smaller tactical targets that can be more easily overcome.

Lesson 5: Your Failure Can Be a Gift for Growth

Ask warriors where they learned the most, and they will point to failures. Failure is a strong reminder that we are human, we mess up, we make mistakes, and we sometimes suffer the consequences. But your most impactful growth comes on the other side of failure—if you look at failure objectively. The warrior is stronger after surviving a failure. The White Collar Warrior is too. Learn to understand that failure will happen. Recognize you have the power to learn from it, and you will emerge stronger, more capable, and with a stronger sense of purpose.

Lesson 6: Your Motivation Matters the Most When You Feel the Worst

It's tough to stay motivated when you are facing a formidable enemy. But motivation is found in the deepest part of your soul. When you connect motivation to your mission and your why, you find the strength you need to pull through. Warriors find their motivation in those fighting next to them.

They are unwilling to let their fellow warriors down. White Collar Warriors persevere for the good of their team, but ultimately, they have a band of brothers—themselves, their families, their friends—who they are unwilling to let down. In the crucible of battle, they dig deep and find the motivation to push on.

Lesson 7: Your Growth Depends on Your Team

There is much you can do to become the best of the best. But driving, striving, and struggling for success is not solely in your hands. Military elite warriors may be the tip of the spear, but they have a vital team that surrounds them on every mission. Each member plays a part, and they all work together to accomplish the mission. In the same way, White Collar Warriors need a team to be the best they can be. Whether you are a lone operator in need of a team to multiply your impact or a leader in charge of a team, developing the people around you will pay dividends in terms of success.

The Path Forward

Each of the next seven chapters will dig deep into these lessons. They will feature a mix of my perspective as a coach, the perspective of a military warrior, and the perspective of successful sales professionals. This mix will provide you with a path forward. Each chapter, as mentioned, ends with a section on "Closing the Gap"—you determine where you are relative to where you want to be. Then create a plan to close the distance between the two. I'll give you questions and action steps at the end of each chapter to help you do three things:

1. **Assess:** This is where you discover your current "battle readiness" in the specific lesson at hand. I'll often provide you with a tool or resource to help you dig deep.
2. **Apply:** These items will help you put into action the things you've learned. It may be a tool, questions, or an activity.
3. **Maintain:** Once you've learned something about yourself and put a plan in place to apply it to your life, you need to continually maintain the process. This keeps you sharp and ready for action.

Preparing for Battle

The Way of the Warrior will provide the resources you need to begin training to become a White Collar Warrior. Granted, your success as a salesperson isn't a life-or-death situation. But what if your attentiveness to preparing today is all that's stopping you from success in the future?

On September 11, 2001, Lieutenant General Mike Wooley, USAF Special Operations Command (retired), experienced firsthand how vital preparation is to success:

> *The more senior that I got, [the more] training meant preparing for battle. When I wound up at Scott Air Force Base on September 11, that training came home in spades. One minute we were in the morning staff meeting, and the executive officer came in and said that an airplane had hit the first tower. We all kind of looked at each other, trying to figure out what was going on. But when he came in and said the*

second airplane hit the second tower, we said, "We're under attack." And we went to work. All that training kicked in, because there was absolutely no time to prepare from that moment on. It was "game on," and the sovereignty of the United States was at stake.

That's what training is all about, for moments like that. It's the same thing with any Special Operations deployment. When they landed those helicopters inside the compound on their mission to kill or capture Osama bin Laden, at that moment in time, you can't think about anything except that mission. **If you are not properly trained and properly rehearsed when the helicopter lands, it's do or die. Literally**.

The truth is, you choose how prepared you are going to be for success. It's up to you. To the best of your ability, commit to the process. Refuse to ring the bell and walk away. Schedule time weekly to go over what you have learned and begin applying it to your life. It's simple but not easy. Becoming the best of the best never is. But the results are worth the effort.

It's not an exaggeration to say that your training could be the difference between the life and death of your career. Do you want to become the kind of person whom others in your field know, respect, and come to for advice and wise counsel? Or do you want to blend in with the masses, keep your head down, and just get by?

I suspect I know which one you are, or you wouldn't be reading this book. Let's get started on our mission together. I'll see you next where all the elite begin—in boot camp.

CHAPTER 3

TRAINING

Lesson 1: Your Training Is the Foundation for Everything

*"The more you sweat in training,
the less you bleed in combat."*

—*Richard Marcinko*

Lieutenant General Mike Wooley knows a few things about what it takes to be the best. As the commander of Air Force Special Operations at Hurlburt Field, Florida, he led a team of more than 12,000 as the Air Force component of US Special Operations command. He's also an experienced pilot who tallied more than 4,400 official hours prior to his retirement from active duty in 2008.

But he didn't start at the top. He first had to learn a critical lesson:

> *I thought I was a hotshot pilot [when
> I started in the US Air Force]. I had a
> couple thousand hours when I went to pilot*

training. When we did the Cessna 172 program, it was a piece of cake for me. I didn't really apply myself.

But then when we got into T-37s [twin-engine jet trainer aircraft], I got into the jet world of checklist discipline. It was about learning everything you can learn about the airplane—what triggers this relay and what does it do? I had to trace every drop of fuel through the entire fuel system and out the exhaust pipe of the engine. I really had to stop and say that it's a wonder I didn't kill myself when I was flying in general aviation, because I really didn't know what aviation was all about.

I remember the first day at pilot training, our wing commander walked up and down the stage giving us the once-over. He had his khakis on and a cigar in his mouth as he went over our training, telling us the rules and what he expected, what he would put up with, and, more importantly, what he wouldn't. I'll summarize what he said like this: "Boys, you all are here for the best aviation career known to man. By my calculations, it's about a six-million-dollar education. My job is to cram it up your ass a nickel at a time."

And that's the way our training started. It was grueling. We played hard and trained hard. But we learned that **training is the foundation for everything**.

A Matter of Life or Death

"Training is the foundation of everything." That's where it all begins for these elite warriors and where it all could very well end. As Lieutenant General Wooley says, the military elite face life-and-death consequences when they fail to train well. There can be no shortcuts.

For the best of the best that our military has to offer, training is very specific and very difficult. The high attrition rates reveal that the training is designed to discover a trainee's point of failure. One Army Ranger told me that there are specific portions of Ranger School that no one can pass. They're designed that way. There are no cheat sheets for the kind of training that introduces you to your own limitations and prepares you to succeed on the battlefield. Leadership and personal growth guru John C. Maxwell says it this way: "Stupid is trying to take shortcuts." Perhaps nowhere is this more evident than in the heat of battle, where shortcuts in training can get you and your comrades killed.

For the elite, what separates success from failure is training. And it never stops for them. Day in and day out, that's what they do. Bob Hart is a US Army Ranger and an experienced flight surgeon. Here is how he describes the never-ending training exercises:

> We are always training. We capitalize on every chance to maximize training opportunities on a daily basis regardless if it is at a training exercise, in garrison, or while deployed. There is no such thing as luck. **Luck is the point in time when preparation and opportunity intersect.**

> *What separates the elite from the rest is not luck. It isn't that they just happened to be in the right place at the right time. Sure, there will always be stuff you can't predict, but effective training prepares you even for the unexpected. The best are always training, always trying to improve themselves, always preparing for whatever might come next.*

As US Army Ranger (retired) Nick Palmisciano points out, most of us overestimate our level of preparation and, therefore, underestimate our need for rigorous training:

> *People tend to be unrealistically confident. Most troops believe they will react correctly, shoot well, and be sufficiently fit. Likewise, most civilians believe they could defend themselves in a fight, most employees think they do a great job, and most businessmen believe their decisions are sound.*
>
> ***They successfully maintain this belief structure because their beliefs go untested.*** *Most soldiers never see combat, most civilians never get into a fight, and most employees and businessmen work for larger corporations with a protective structure in place.* ***It is only when people are challenged and forced to deal with reality that the truth of their preparedness becomes apparent***.

Think about it: most of us think we could do a lot of things—if we had to. We tell ourselves we *could* be the best salesperson ever *if* we really wanted to. But there is a significant difference between thinking we can and knowing we can. The military elite cannot afford to live with that gap. They cannot assume they are ready. They need to know they are ready *before* bullets start flying. They must be honest with themselves about themselves. It's a matter of life and death.

Why Training Matters to You

So it must be with you, the sales professional desiring to be the best. You may think you will be ready to succeed when opportunity knocks, but how do you know? Are you really trained well enough, or do you just think you're ready? My friend Tom Ferry, a highly successful real estate coach, says, "Let's face it, for the vast majority of us, our heads are a very scary place to be. I never met a salesperson that didn't have some ambitions, some drive, and some desire to make more money, help more clients, and achieve something. But what gets in the way the most is right between our ears." People who value training are people who are honest with themselves. If you're not sure, ask yourself this question: what do your results say about your level of preparation? Do the numbers you're producing right now accurately portray you at your best? If not, take a look at your training. Training is the foundation of everything, including your sales results.

You may think you are ready. But remember what Army Ranger Nick Palmisciano said: "People tend to be unrealistically confident…because their beliefs go untested." Let's face it—reality can be a tough teacher. Heavyweight boxer Mike Tyson once said, "Everyone has a plan until they get punched in the mouth." The good news for you is that your tests in the sales world will likely *not* include fists and bullets (though

I suppose that could depend on what you are selling, and where). But you do need to test yourself, to stretch yourself and discover the truth about you and what you can do when your training kicks in.

When we don't train well, we lack the confidence to act. Instead, we do what comes naturally. We duck situations that test our ability. We dodge scenarios that might expose our lack of training. We often call it "call reluctance" or "call aversion." It's understandable. None of us enjoy finding out we aren't ready. But avoiding the truth will only sabotage our sales efforts. When opportunity knocks at the front door, we're already slipping out the back because we're just not ready.

Robert M. Pirsig describes this avoidance behavior when he says, "It's a puzzling thing. The truth knocks on the door and you say, 'Go away, I'm looking for the truth.' And so it goes away. Puzzling." Training introduces you to yourself, to your limits and your strengths. It reveals the truth about you. Perhaps that's why most of us avoid it. We say we want to grow, but really, we don't want to know the truth about ourselves. So we fail to train well, preferring to think we *could* rise to the occasion in a crisis if we really wanted to.

The truth is that you must train for moments of crisis (or opportunity), whether you're rappelling from a Blackhawk helicopter in Afghanistan or sharing an elevator with the CEO of a company you've been trying to sell to for the past five years. And it is in moments of crisis, when opportunity presents itself, that can make all the difference. Only the well-trained can seize them.

Have you ever envied other sales professionals who seem to always be in the right place at the right time? Some call that luck—but not the elite. As Army Ranger Bob Hart says, luck doesn't just happen for the elite. Luck is what happens when our training takes advantage of an opportunity.

Back to Basic Training

The thing about training is that when it comes right down to it, it really isn't all that complicated. That's the good news. Anyone can do it.

We tend to spend a lot of time looking for that one extra insight that will give us an edge or a magical way of asking that will close the deal. But Bob Hart describes training for the elite in a decidedly unglamorous fashion: "We focus on basic skills and add complexity once the foundation is solid. Without a solid foundation, advanced skills are negligible. **Rangers pride themselves on being the masters of the basics.**"

In my experience, most salespeople want to soar with the best, but they train like the rest. They want to go to BUD/S training, but they haven't completed basic training. They want to fly F-117 stealth fighters without first learning the mechanics of fuel flow on the Cessna trainer. They want to be put where the action is, but they're so out of shape that they wouldn't last more than ten minutes once their boots hit the ground.

Training conditions you to do three basic things essential for success in sales: think. Speak. Act. (In the military, a basic training tenet is, "Shoot. Move. Communicate.") Let's unpack those three areas of training together to see where you need to make changes.

What You Think

For the military elite, the real battle is won in the mind, before they ever begin to condition themselves and long before their boots ever touch the ground or their fins feel the frigid ocean currents. Every candidate for Navy SEAL BUD/S training is physically fit—far more than you or I will ever be—but that is not enough to succeed. It takes a mental discipline that is a step above to survive and thrive. Marcus Luttrell recalls these words burned into him by Chief Petty Officer Bob Nielsen just prior to beginning training:

> *He closed by telling us the real battle is won in the mind. It's won by guys who understand their areas of weakness, who sit and think about it, plotting and planning to improve. Attending to the detail. Work on their weaknesses and overcome them. Because they can.*

And so can you. I don't know about you, but I find it freeing and empowering to learn that I am in control of what will determine my own success. There's a lot in life I can't control—the market, the weather, traffic, just to name a few. But I can do a lot about what goes on inside my own head. In fact, I'm just about the only person who can. What goes on inside of you is far and away the leading factor in determining your success. Remember Army Ranger Chad Fleming? His take on training is, "There is just no question that the physical is only 10 percent—inner drive is 90 percent."

Andrew Paul also knows a thing or two about sales as the leader of a highly successful mortgage brokerage firm in Southern California. After leaving active duty, Andrew became a loan officer and dedicated himself to helping his fellow veterans use their VA Loan benefits. Here's his take on an essential way of training how we think:

*At an early point in my life, I was fascinated with the SEALs. They were shrouded in mystery, a group that was only for the best. The more I was told no, the more I wanted it. I prepared for years to become a SEAL—prepared to be tough! But BUD/S is so physically demanding; sooner or later everyone's body will break down. **What I learned is that you must be mentally tough**.*

*My defining moment was during Hell Week, the lowest I've ever been in my life. I remember looking at a friend. We each acknowledged the pain. From that point forward, I was untouchable. Whatever they did, I was unphased. Growing physically is one thing, but during Hell Week, I grew mentally. Growing mentally is amazing. We do physical training over and over again, but **the true warrior is most powerful who has the mindset**. The inexperienced don't recognize that yet and may never recognize it.*

*It's really all about mindset, knowing that victory is always possible one way or another eventually. **It's about deciding to never quit—to never accept defeat**.*

Another American hero is Sean Parnell, an Army Ranger and veteran of 485 days of fierce fighting along the Afghan-Pakistan border. He led a platoon that was repeatedly outnumbered and outgunned in some of the most rugged terrain on the planet. Sean was wounded in action on June 10, 2006, when his platoon was nearly overrun for the first time by a force that outnumbered them almost ten to one. He authored the *New York Times* bestseller *Outlaw Platoon* to tell the story of those brave men.

The value of his training was proven repeatedly under fire against overwhelming odds. Here is what he shared with me about the value of training the right mindset:

> *Ranger School taught me that my body is capable of a hell of a lot more than what that voice in my head tells me it's capable of. I went to Ranger School weighing 210 pounds and running six-minute-thirty-seconds miles without a pound of fat on my body. I was in the best shape of my life. I left training at 150 pounds, and I learned that it's not about the physical shape that you're in; **it's about a mindset of never quitting**.*
>
> *I had a roommate in college that was in much better shape than I was. We went to Ranger School—I made it; he didn't. I graduated Ranger School with trench foot in both feet and two broken feet. I had lost sixty pounds. I was emaciated, starving, and hallucinating. What I learned is that it is a mindset, a mental thing in Ranger School. Can you go further than anybody else around you?*
>
> *Your physical condition doesn't matter, because after a month, everybody's in the same shape. Everyone has lost their mus-*

> cle. *Everyone is starving. In those moments where you are hurting worse than you have ever hurt in your life, your brain will say, "You don't need to be a Ranger—just stop this. Go home and eat." For me, Ranger School was all about telling myself, "I am not going to leave here without becoming a Ranger." **It's a mindset. You have to make up your mind before you even go in.***

One way I coach sales professionals to think differently is by adopting what I call the "I Have a Responsibility" Mindset. My son-in-law is a physician who feels it is his responsibility to advise friends and family of a simple but life-transforming truth: *If you want to get sick less, wash your hands more.* And—he's always quick to add—sing "Happy Birthday" while washing to ensure you wash them long enough to do some serious good. Marc has a sense of responsibility when it comes to that information; he sees himself as a caretaker of that message and shares it with others every chance he gets. He'll also have a meaningful conversation with you about the overuse of antibiotics, but that's a story for another day.

In the same way, when a sales professional frames thoughts about a customer within a responsibility mindset, it becomes a privileged duty to listen, advise, and then consult with or educate the customer. When he or she takes responsibility, the interaction often results in a win for the customer. And a win for the customer increases the likelihood of a win for the salesperson. Consequently, it's not the allure of a commission that drives the interaction, but a genuine sense of responsibility for seeing the customer's needs met.

Any sales professional is going to have to learn how to deal with an objection, which sometimes turns into a rejection. When you train for these objections and you think about the customer through the lens of the "I Have a Responsibility" Mindset, objections aren't obstacles, and rejection is never final. When you consider your role—to become a trusted partner in the process—you acknowledge that objection, come alongside as a guide, and educate them. An example might sound like this:

"I can totally see how you might feel that way."

(Acknowledge)

"If I were in your shoes, I think I might as well. Here's something to consider…"

(Educate)

"Can you see how this would benefit you in your situation?"

(Call to action)

Well-trained salespeople anticipate objections and have a plan to deal with them. They aren't formulaic in their responses. They acknowledge the person's feelings so the objection doesn't become a divider to their relationship. When you are genuine and look out for your customer's needs, you become an ally. You aren't one of many salespeople pushing your version of the product or service. You're a partner vested in the client's success, happiness, and ultimate benefit.

The best way to overcome resistance to prospecting is to flip the switch in your head. Change the thought of "What's in it for me?" to "How will this benefit them?" Down the road, you may get something from it, but don't let that be your primary motivation. Tom Ferry says, "I believe sales is the ability to ask a series of questions that naturally and automatically lead my prospect and me to a mutually desired end result. The only victory is when we both win, and sometimes winning means it's a no!" The best salespeople who experience long-term success are those who determine to bring value to the client, customer, or market first.

And in the process of doing so, they get paid.

What You Say

Don't let your training stop with what lies between your ears. You must train those thoughts to come out of your mouth as the right words. Remember: you'll always avoid putting yourself in a position where you lack confidence to perform. Until you know what you will say and how you will say it—and have rehearsed it until it's second nature—you'll tend to dodge the very conversations you need to succeed.

My best man at my wedding taught me the importance of knowing what to say. No, he didn't have to give me any hints during the ceremony, but Harold Dyck was also the director of training for Century 21 Real Estate in Southern California when we worked together in the '80s. I helped people get a real estate license, and Harold trained them. Harold taught a new class every month called "Two and One." The idea was to help real estate salespeople produce two listings and one sale every month.

But the class was a revolving door because the vast majority of attendees never averaged two listings and one sale per month. Harold believed the new recruits would be more likely to engage in conversations with prospective clients if he could convince them to learn what to say and what to ask. He was absolutely right. He would start by teaching them a "listing presentation," training them for the conversation they would inevitably have with a prospective seller. Harold was convinced beyond a shadow of a doubt that if salespeople didn't know what to say when they were in front of a prospective seller, they would avoid the listing conversation altogether. Almost without exception, the students who trained well sold well.

Knowing what to say and rehearsing how to say it will give you the confidence you need to run *toward* sales situations instead of running *away* from them.

I'm not a fan of memorizing scripts and dialogues, but I am a fan of being prepared and knowing where to go in predictable situations in sales. Navy SEALs and Army Rangers don't memorize exact physical moves or tactics; they master certain elements to deploy, in a natural and organic way, in every situation. In the same way, the best sales professionals do have arrows in their quiver for the most common objections:

"We're really just shopping around."

"We can get it for less somewhere else."

"We'd like to think about it."

I call them *bulletized* responses (and given the military analogy, it works). They empower the sales professional to deploy the right words in the right situation as needed. Bulletize your responses to predictable objections and let your amazing brain weave them into sentences that sound natural and free-flowing rather than stilted and rehearsed.

Bulletized responses also have the benefit of helping bring your authenticity to life. Remember that the best salespeople build authentic relationships that add value to and benefit the customer (or potential customer). If you've worked hard to cultivate that relationship to a point where the customer knows and trusts you, a scripted response is going to come across as unnatural. I recently posted a question on Facebook: "How Do You Respond to 'Your Price Is Too High?'" There were many well-thought-out responses, primarily around investment versus cost and apples-to-apples comparisons, but the one that stood out the most was from my twenty-one-year-old grandson. He chimed in by saying to some of the more formulaic "I learned this in sales training" responses that it sounded to him like "word salad." That can't be good.

Bulletizing your responses allows you to cover potential questions or objections but use your own words to do so. Your authenticity will shine through in a way that is endearing and even further strengthens your relationship.

Have you ever seen a politician give a speech and rely too heavily on the teleprompter? You could almost see his or her eyes reading the words on the screen. It can be the best speech in the world, but if the speaker relies too heavily on the script, the authenticity disappears and it looks like what it is—a person reading words on a page.

The old-school way of responding to objections was to have scripted responses for every possible customer objection. If your goal is to get one sale, then this approach may work. Have you ever purchased a car from an automotive dealership? The traditional (old school) salespeople know they have one chance to get you to buy. If you walk out that door, you aren't coming back. They also know that you won't be back to buy a second car the following week. So they focus on the one sale at hand. This is a highly transactional business, so the scripted responses work great. You raise an objection, and they come back with a canned response. It buys time and keeps you on the lot. (Thankfully, increasingly, this is changing in car dealerships as more car buyers start their purchase process online.)

But if your goal is to build a long-term relationship with your customers, you need a more organic approach. They don't expect you to be perfect; they expect you to be real. They don't expect you to be just like some other great salesperson to whom you may be comparing yourself. They expect you to be you. Don't try to be like everyone else. They're taken. Be you. As Dr Seuss famously said: "Today you are You, that is truer than true. There is no one alive who is Youer than You."

Authenticity advocate Greg Cagle says that the best of the best don't try to be like everyone else. They embrace their "weirdness." He says your weirdness makes you unique, and your uniqueness is the key to greatness. Your natural strengths are what make you relatable. So rely on those and be natural and at ease with your customers. This is easy to do when you use the bulletized response method. It also ensures that they'll call you or pick up your call, over and over again.

I do a good bit of video sharing and teaching in my business, and I often use the bulletized response method as I record video. I write out a list of bullet points that I want to be sure to cover. Of course these are familiar to me, because I've spent time in advance thinking about what I want to say. When I record video, I keep those bullet points off to the side, where I can glance at them and mentally check each one off as I record. As I visualize a bullet point, I mentally retrieve what I want to say, and I teach or speak that lesson intuitively. It doesn't sound exactly like what I wrote down, and that's a good thing. Instead it matches the pace and tone of the rest of the video and authentically conveys my points in real time.

The best speakers do this too. They survey the room, gather the clues from the audience, and deliver their message in a way that the audience relates to. They don't change their message, but they do modify it as needed to make the biggest impact. I know as an experienced presenter what lines connect or elicit specific, desired responses, and make a note to repeat them next time.

Bulletized responses empower you to cover the objections and questions that arise in a way that is natural and well-thought-out. Holly Reed, who has become incredibly successful at Rodan & Fields Skincare, told me when she started, "I began to listen to the people who were there before me and who had found success. I began to listen to their language, listen to their approach, and try to get into an understanding of their daily activity. I knew to succeed I needed to become a student of the industry." Spend some time thinking about your specific industry and what objections or questions consistently pop up. Brainstorm on a page a list of the best responses that answer each question and overcome each objection. I would craft the best sentences I could think of that set a client's mind at ease. Write yours down and read them over and over. As you review these responses in your head, they will become ingrained in your subconscious. It's a form of mental training that connects what you think with what you say. Then highlight a specific word or phrase that can become a bulletized response.

For each product or service you sell or represent, create a list of these bulletized responses. Start at the beginning and craft the best possible version of your response until it becomes lodged firmly in your mind. Then turn those sentences into short bullets that you can recall on a moment's notice. Just like soldiers use muscle memory to bring their weapon up to face a threat, you can quickly pull your bulletized responses up at a moment's notice to counter any objections you may face. The more you do it, the more natural it will become. And the more natural it becomes, the greater your capacity for productive and profitable sales will be.

What You Do

If we train only our minds and voices, we will still fall short. We have to actually do something to complete the mission. We must practice what to do in order to do what we want under pressure in the moment. Ranger Nick Palmisciano puts it plainly:

> ***Ultimately, how you train is how you execute.*** *If you can't shoot at a range, you won't be able to hit with any level of consistency the enemy who is shooting back while adrenaline runs through your body. If you've never been punched or never punched someone, you will not successfully defend yourself against an attacker. If you haven't mastered your business and constantly challenged yourself to learn more and improve skills and processes, you will never*

be able to succeed as an entrepreneur outside
the confines of a corporate shell.

Members of the military elite talk a lot about *muscle memory*, doing the right things so often that their bodies remember what to do without conscious thought. Right thinking and rehearsing should lead us to take the right action—again and again. The goal is to get so used to doing the right thing that our minds are free to fully engage in opportunity. Ranger Bob Hart describes the physical portion of his training in this way:

> *Combat physical conditioning was less complex. Early training focused more on simple muscle memory or response; however, as skills and knowledge base improved, the training shifted more towards **creative problem-solving, reaction to increased stress, improvisation, and complex decisions** that would often result in second- and third-order effects.*

One of the best ways I've found to establish this muscle memory with my coaching clients is by role-playing. Role-playing combines mental training with actions turned into muscle memory. You may have read a particular sales book and jotted down notes in the margin or underlined key passages that stood out to you. But how do you get those words off the page and into action? One way that works well is to sit down with a trusted friend—someone on your side (the military jargon is "friendlies")—and work together to drill those concepts into your subconscious.

Role-playing with a friendly forces you to consider what you've read or learned and think critically about it. It's like picking up a diamond and considering it from all sides. As you turn it over in your hand, you feel each facet with your fingertips. Your eyes see the clarity and sparkle. Sitting with a friendly who actively probes you with questions or spins specific scenarios forces you to see things from all the angles. When you do this, you condition your mind to react automatically. You create a neural pathway and, eventually, a habit.

In his book *Getting Things Done*, David Allen uses the phrase "mind like water." He's referring to the discipline of martial arts in which it is said that water reacts appropriately based on what you do to it. If you throw a small pebble, you get a small splash. If you throw a brick, you get a larger splash. Allen says in martial arts you learn that if you're in a dark alley and five guys attack you, you should let your mind become like water. React naturally, without a great deal of thought. In that moment, you don't want to think, *OK, so what I'm gonna do is move toward him and I'm gonna punch him and then I'm gonna try and turn around and kick him before that other guy picks up the baseball bat.* You don't want those thoughts going on in your head; you just need to react and follow your instincts. Mind like water.

This is what role-playing does for you. Role-playing puts you into a scenario where you simulate the situation in practice so that when you're in the real situation, your subconscious says, "I've been here before." In the military, trainers now teach small-arms combat tactics using lasers and wax ammunition ("simunition"). They put soldiers in simulated combat situations, ratchet up the pressure, and practice firing and fighting. These high-definition and highly equipped laser sensors and laser rifles get our military members as close to combat as possible without putting them in danger. Of course, it doesn't have all the pressure of live fire, but that's the point. They train in the safety of simulated combat so when the bullets start flying, their bodies and minds know what to do. They've been there before. Mind like water.

In sales, you obviously aren't facing a life-or-death situation. But the same principles apply. Take what you are doing seriously in training, and that training will come back to guide you during the "live fire" of a sales call or presentation. You won't worry about what you are doing, because you've been there before. You know how it will play out.

The best role-playing is obviously done with another human being. The best choice is a person who is your peer and who understands the industry and objections you will face. These friendlies will help you to become your best by forcing you to leave no stone unturned. An additional benefit of role-playing with a peer is that you sharpen one another. As you take turns practicing what you'll do in a real situation, you see both sides of the sales process. This will take root in your mind and come out when you least expect it.

Don't get too hung up on the method of role-playing. It can be as simple as asking someone to listen to your presentation and give you feedback. Be willing to take constructive criticism and make adjustments as needed. Wise servicemembers don't get offended when their commanding officers give them wisdom that will save their lives in battle! They file it away, apply what they've learned, and fight on. Encourage the person who is helping you to ask pointed questions that force you to think on your feet. Be willing to admit you don't know, and then go find the answer. It will only strengthen your presentation when you take it live.

The Power of Habit

So why go through the work of role-playing and practicing until you know things backward and forward? Simple. You want to establish a habit. Role-playing trains you in a way that creates habits. You no longer think; you react. In his book *The One Thing*, author Gary Keller proposes that 10 percent of success comes from classwork, 20 percent comes from shadowing, and 70 percent comes from experience. The best way to gain experience before a battle is by role-playing until your reactions become habits.

Habits are powerful because they help us work more efficiently. When you work more efficiently, you become more effective. When you become more effective, you become a better salesperson. A well-trained salesperson—like a well-trained servicemember—is prepared for the rigors he or she will face, whether on the battlefield or in the business office.

In *The Power of Habit: Why We Do What We Do in Life and in Business*, author Charles Duhigg identifies what he calls "the habit loop." He says:

> *Habits aren't destiny. Habits can be ignored, changed, or replaced. But the reason the discovery of the habit loop is so important is that it reveals a basic truth:* **When a habit emerges, the brain stops fully participating in decision-making.** *It stops working so hard, or diverts focus to other tasks. So unless you deliberately fight a habit—unless you find new routines—the pattern will unfold automatically.*

As he describes it, the habit loop is composed of three elements: cue, routine, and reward. If you lay out your running shoes and workout clothes at night before bed, then that is the *cue* you see first thing in the morning. You automatically move into your workout *routine* and finally *reward* yourself with the knowledge that you completed the workout and a healthy smoothie.

If you create your very own habit loop around prospecting, it will pay huge dividends. Here's a simple way for you to create a sales call *cue*. Break down your goals into the number of calls you need to make each day, either in person or by phone. Then post that number somewhere where you are sure to see it as you calibrate your day.

The best approach for getting into the *routine* of making calls is to a) schedule them and b) be accountable to someone. Accountability for most is the game-changer and one of the best reasons to enlist the support of a coach. But you can choose to be accountable to anyone. That place in your brain where you manufacture excuses is most effective when there's no one else in there with you. You'll find a way to explain away why it didn't happen today, and you'll "double up tomorrow." Yeah, right. Not likely. An accountability partner will likely call you on it and I guarantee you that a good coach will.

The *reward* for making your calls can be whatever works for you. Maybe it's sipping a latte, playing a sport, or relaxing by the pool. Hitting golf balls at the driving range is a great mental escape and decompression time for me. That's often my payoff after I've done something difficult for me, like writing or creating a presentation for an upcoming talk. Choose what works for you, and give yourself something to look forward to after you respond to the cue and engage the routine.

It's important to remember that this cue-reward-routine cycle also works in the negative sense. Stress is a perfect example. If stress from a long day at work is your cue, you can choose to respond to it by opening up a bottle of Jack Daniels and pouring yourself a nice, strong drink every night. You've got the same process going on, it's the habit loop, but it's destructive. You're anesthetizing yourself, you're not connecting with your family, and you fall asleep having put a depressant in your body. If you could replace that destructive habit with a constructive habit, like taking a twenty-minute walk, you would rewire that habit loop to cause positive changes.

You may have developed some bad habits around your work and sales processes that need to be changed. The end of this chapter will provide an exercise to help you determine where those bad habits are and make a plan to turn them around. Just like a chain is only as strong as its weakest link, your success is strengthened by your good habits and sabotaged by your bad habits.

When basic sales skills become our basic daily habits, we're ready to tackle greater challenges and seize opportunities as they arise. It may be something as simple as rolling out of bed before dawn and reviewing your life and business plan. It may mean staying physically fit so you have the energy to engage prospects more fully. Or it could mean promptly following up with networking opportunities after a social event. The elite agree: whatever actions are basic to your success need to become habits—part of your muscle memory, requiring no great thought, only intentional action.

Ranger Bob Hart says this about the connection between the mental and physical:

*Operationally, both types of training [mental and physical] are absolutely required to provide care to combat casualties in an austere environment. Brute strength does no good if you are mentally weak and do not possess the knowledge base and critical problem-solving skills required to make life-or-death decisions for casualties. Ranger medics must be both physically and mentally capable. We train and push ourselves harder than anything we will see in combat **so that even complex tasks are muscle memory and come naturally in all circumstances**, and can be done in the pitch-black dead of night under the worst conditions.*

Closing the Gap

Assess

• What situations do you avoid that might expose your lack of training? What opportunities are knocking at the front door while you're sneaking out the back? Write down some times when you know you have avoided opportunities. Bulletizing scripting? Learning that new technology? An opportunity to speak to a group? Based on that information, what does it look like you need training in the most?

_____

_____

_____

_____

_____

- When did you last participate in professional training? Has it been months? Years? Many professions (doctors, teachers, pilots, and so on) require ongoing training to maintain certification, but sales professionals often must fend for themselves. If you don't have a plan, schedule time in your calendar this week to research training options—then commit to at least one of them.

_____

_____

_____

_____

_____

Apply

- According to Zig Ziglar, "The most influential person you will talk to all day is you." When you make excuses all day, that conversation with yourself could be a problem. Find an accountability partner, someone who isn't you, who will call you out if you back down from training goals. Think of some people who might fill this role, and set up a conversation with one of them to enlist their help. Send that person a text NOW.

_____

_____

_____

_____

_____

- Think of someone in your industry whose professional style you admire. Why not schedule a lunch meeting with him or her to get advice on training? People love to talk about what works for them, so listen carefully and then act accordingly. Modeling is powerful!

_____

_____

_____

_____

_____

MAINTAIN

- Teaching others can actually be a powerful learning tool, forcing you to think specifically about what has and has not worked for you. Do you know anyone just coming up in the business who could benefit from what you know? You never learn anything as well as when you have to teach it, as the saying goes. Step into that truth. Reach out to someone today who might enjoy having a conversation with someone more experienced—you.

_____

_____

_____

_____

_____

- Time for a habit check! You probably have a mix of bad and good ones. Make a list of the bad habits you know you have. Then using Duhigg's habit loop, sketch out concrete ways to turn those negative habits into positive ones. Be as specific as possible to ensure you can track your progress.

_____

_____

_____

_____

_____

CHAPTER 4

DISCIPLINE

Lesson 2: Your Discipline Will Determine Your Success

"We must all suffer from one of two pains: the pain of discipline or the pain of regret. The difference is, discipline weighs ounces while regret weighs tons."

—Jim Rohn

I often have my clients memorize that quote and recite it to me in our next coaching session. The beauty of it is that once it's in your head—it's in. Few people enjoy the pain of discipline. But the best of the best have learned to overcome the temporary pain of discipline to reap the rewards of focused effort. Disciplined action leads to consistent results. And consistent results are the benchmark of success. Discipline is having the integrity to put your training into action, especially in the face of adversity. It is part of who you are—but it can also be learned.

In the military, good discipline isn't just a benchmark of success; it's often a matter of life or death. Maintaining discipline under fire is what keeps your team alive. Lieutenant General Wooley told me this about discipline:

> ***If you are not disciplined to do exactly what you're trained to do, you could be responsible for the death of your teammates around you.*** *So discipline is one of those foundational things that has to be ingrained from day one. You've got to act instinctively with discipline to make sure that you carry out the mission at hand.*
>
> *We've got countless examples of this, where Air Force combat controllers have been wounded and are sitting there bleeding, and they rip open one of their clotting bandages and hold it up to their sucking chest wound as they're calling in an Air Evac airplane to pick up their wounded teammates. And shortly behind that, calls for fire from an A-10 to help assist getting them out, or calling in an AC-130, or even calling in another C-130 that has a paramedic or a helicopter with a PJ [Pararescue jumper] on it, to have him jump in to do lifesaving measures.*
>
> *All of that takes discipline. You know, he could pretty much just lie there and ask for help himself, but it's the discipline, respect, and the love for his team members to keep focused on the job at hand.*

Ranger Nick Palmisciano echoes Mike's praise for discipline—especially now that Nick is an entrepreneur concerned with sales:

> *Discipline has made all the difference in my life, especially now as an entrepreneur. People think that success comes overnight. That is rarely the truth. People succeed by trying, failing, learning, and trying again. You have to have the discipline to continue to work, continue to attack the problems that arise, and continue to improve incrementally.* ***Discipline keeps you from quitting, and in my experience that is the most important element of success****, greater even than natural ability, intelligence, or even the quality of one's initial idea.*

For the sales professional, discipline is just as vital. Perhaps no other field has as much leeway as sales. Think about it. You are primarily accountable to only yourself. A sales manager or an executive may check in on you, but only periodically. You likely set your own schedule, have your own routine for making prospecting calls, and decide how long and how hard you're going to work. It's easy to be comfortable.

Most people don't like to be uncomfortable, but discipline is all about being uncomfortable. So in the same way that you don't want to run, because you don't want to get sweaty and sore, you may not want to prospect either. It's hard work. You'll face a lot of rejection, and it's easier to coast.

Just as people who refuse to exercise say it's easier to sit on the couch with a bag of potato chips, undisciplined sales professionals make excuses too. They look over their prospect list one more time (without making a call). They ask colleagues what methods have been working for them. They check Facebook to see if they can make any new networking contacts. They head to a 3 p.m. meeting and then head home because it's been such a challenging day. Perhaps it sounds harsh, but these excuses have a way of adding up over time and derailing any chance of success. Discipline is tough, but the alternative is much tougher.

The Weight of Discipline

In your life, you will carry burdens. That's just part of the privilege of living. But you get to choose the weight of those burdens and when to carry them.

Discipline, practiced daily, weighs only ounces. Sure, it's not much fun at the time to sweat and exercise, but if you want to live a long, healthy life, you get on the treadmill or pick up those weights and put in your time. It's not always fun to cultivate relationships with sales contacts and face rejection phone call after phone call. But the law of averages and time and consistency will prevail. If you want to build a financially strong base, you have to put in the work.

The pain of regret, however, is a burden that no one wants to carry. It is crushing and debilitating, because it's impossible to go back and fix it. Those moments of unhealthy living often cannot be undone, and those bad habits from long ago can shorten, or even end, your life. Failing to cultivate long-term, mutually beneficial sales relationships today will affect your livelihood tomorrow. Either way, you're going to experience pain. So which is better? Identify the disciplines that you're going to commit to and get done what you need to get done. The good news is that countless people before you have developed a disciplined lifestyle and harvested the benefits. There's no reason you can't do the same—one decision at a time.

The Power of Accountability

Discipline has a close relative that is just as ignored by many but every bit as important. In fact, to truly harness the power of discipline, it must be hitched to this other word—*accountability*. Accountability is a catalyst for success. Accountability means you open yourself up to another person's connection or observation and empower that person to keep you on track.

As a coach, providing accountability is one of my core functions. Most people know the right thing to do. You know you should exercise to keep healthy, but you hire a personal trainer to kick you in the butt and make you do the workouts. You are smart enough to learn anything you put your mind to, but you pay for college or continuing education training classes so you have skin in the game. My clients are smart enough to have an intuitive sense of what they need to do, but they hire me to provide them with a second set of eyes and a strong voice to keep them on track. When people ask me what coaching is, I tell them it's three things:

- Helping clients to get clear on what they really want personally and professionally.
- Creating mutually agreed-upon action plans that will close the gaps between where they are and where they want to be.
- Having accountability for what they said they would do.

In coaching, accountability invariably turns vague ideas into a focused plan. Once we've determined a mutually agreeable action plan, we'll turn to the issue of accountability. If clients tell me they really need more accountability, for example, I'll ask them to text me at the end of every day to tell me how many sales calls they made or miles they've run.

Discipline is like the sinew of the muscle that creates the opportunity—it's the synapse between intentionality and result. Discipline makes it happen. There are plenty of people in the sales world who say they want success, but there are far fewer who make it happen. The difference between good intentions and intentionality is discipline. The people who say, "I'm all-in. Let's go. Show me what to do. I'll make the calls. I'll come back bloody, battered, and disappointed, but I'll come back and do it the next day" are the people who, over time, are going to get the results. Of course, it's not the saying…it's the doing.

Discipline separates the dreamers from the doers.

First Things First–Make Your Bed

In his commencement speech to the 2014 graduating class of the University of Texas, Admiral William McRaven gave a simple yet profound example of the power of discipline. McRaven honed his discipline to a high level when he became a US Navy SEAL, but he first learned the power of discipline through the simple act of making his bed:

> *Every morning in basic SEAL training, my instructors, who at the time were all Vietnam veterans, would show up in my barracks room, and the first thing they would inspect*

was your bed. If you did it right, the corners would be square, the covers pulled tight, the pillow centered just under the headboard, and the extra blanket folded neatly at the foot of the rack.

It was a simple task—mundane at best. But every morning we were required to make our bed to perfection. It seemed a little ridiculous at the time, particularly in light of the fact that we were aspiring to be real warriors—tough, battle-hardened SEALs— but the wisdom of this simple act has been proven to me many times over.

If you make your bed every morning, you will have accomplished the first task of the day. It will give you a small sense of pride, and it will encourage you to do another task and another and another. By the end of the day, that one task completed will have turned into many tasks completed. Making your bed will also reinforce the fact that little things in life matter.

If you can't do the little things right, you will never do the big things right. *And if by chance you have a miserable day, you will come home to a bed that is made— that you made—and a made bed gives you encouragement that tomorrow will be better.*

If you want to change the world, start off by making your bed.

The most disciplined and successful salespeople know to put first things first. They do the little things well so that big things aren't so big. They also know a secret—being disciplined in the little things builds momentum. It's like a snowball rolling downhill. It starts out small and slowly, but then it picks up momentum and gains size. Soon it can't be stopped.

Disciplined sales professionals recognize that they are playing the long game, and by doing the small things right each day, they set themselves up for future success. Embrace the grind that produces results and realize that you are running a marathon, not a sprint.

Paying the Price

One of my coaching clients once told me he was going to have to get a home equity line of credit on his house to improve his cash flow and help pay the bills after he took two months off for vacation. He's a wonderful guy, larger than life and enormously likable. But he pays me to speak the truth, so I reminded him that his bills should be paid for with the income produced by his daily activities that lead to results. I gently told him that instead of staying disciplined and putting first things first, he'd been on several vacations that put him in a financial bind. I asked him if he agreed that mindset needed to stop.

Of course, I wasn't telling him anything he didn't already know, but he agreed that he needed to get his priorities in order and pay the price that discipline required. Together we came up with a simple plan. He would build in the discipline that he was going to proactively make calls for an hour a day. Two weeks later, he started to build momentum. He called me and said, "I figured it out. I'm a salesman. And that means an

hour a day is nonsense. I should be doing that all the time!"
After just two weeks of disciplined intentionality, he had built
up momentum and exceeded his own expectations.

It's amazing how disciplined you can become when your
back is against the wall. When excuses fall away and you dig
down deep—that's when momentum grows. Is there a price
to pay? Absolutely, but remember Jim Rohn's quote. Would
you rather carry the weight of ounces now or tons later?

Remember Max Leaman, the highly successful mortgage
banker who talked about winning? In my interview with Max,
he made an interesting connection between motivation and
discipline. At first, Max said he didn't really consider himself disciplined, but he did consider himself highly motivated.
This seemed somewhat incongruous, since he was managing
three cell phone stores at the age of nineteen and later became
one of the highest-producing loan officers in the country. But
the more we talked, the more Max connected his motivation
to his discipline and ultimately to his success:

> It's interesting…I've never really thought of
> myself as being disciplined. I've always kind
> of thought of myself as being motivated.
> But I think if you really think about it,
> **being motivated and disciplined, they
> probably go hand in hand**. Again, I've
> always been motivated and disciplined to be
> the best at whatever I'm doing.

So what is it that motivates you? If you discover what that
is, you can pivot that motivation into a disciplined routine
that takes you where you want to go. Like Max, you may not
have ever considered yourself disciplined, but you probably
have a list of daily or monthly routines that you've used to help

you achieve your goals. Discipline matters. When you can connect it to your motivations, you multiply its effectiveness.

From the coach's chair, I have clearly seen that discipline is *the* difference-maker that separates the average producer from the exceptional one. In the world of sales, everything matters. It matters when you wake up and when you go to bed. It matters what you eat, what you drink, and how much. It matters whom you call and what you say when you call. It matters how many prospects you identify. On the flip side, it matters how much time you spend on nonproductive, brain-numbing activities. The choices you make each day will determine your effectiveness. The right small choices, made every day, will lead to exponential success. I've seen it time and again with my clients. Discipline changes things, one choice at a time.

Discipline Equals Freedom

Maybe at this point, you're on the fence. Some part of you gets what I'm saying and you know that being disciplined is the right thing to do, but you just don't want to be handcuffed by discipline. You like to react and respond as necessary. Let me tell you about Jocko.

Jocko Willink led SEAL teams in Iraq and ultimately commanded the West Coast SEAL teams. He looks exactly like what you'd imagine a battle-hardened Special Forces operator named Jocko to look like: buzzed head, craggy face, neck the size of one of my thighs, a perpetual scowl, and icy blue eyes. Since he retired from active duty, he has established a consulting business, cowritten a book called *Extreme Ownership*, started a highly successful podcast, and developed a massive following on social media. He has a simple mantra that he lives by: *discipline equals freedom.*

Every morning Jocko posts a picture of his watch on social media with phrases like "get some," "attack," "no quarter," and "do the work." He's up before 4:30 a.m. seizing the day, every day.

Discipline equals freedom has become a brand. What Jocko has learned is that discipline isn't constraining; it actually frees you to do the things you want to do. He says, "Because I'm disciplined with my workouts, I have the freedom to do some of the things physically that I might not be able to do if I weren't in good shape. Because I'm disciplined financially, I have the freedom to be able to make decisions and choices that I might not be able to otherwise."

People often gravitate to the sales world because of the perceived freedom. You get to be your own boss and do what you want to do. No constraints. But Jocko says that in order to get freedom, you must get disciplined. So if you're disciplined to make your calls, connections, and follow-ups, you'll get great results and the freedom that comes with success.

Most people push back on that (remember, most people are not the elite). *Whoa, dude! I don't want to be disciplined. I just want to be free.* Discipline equals freedom. *Discipline* is an unattractive word. People don't like it. They don't want to be disciplined in how they eat. They don't want to be disciplined in their approach to their business. But in the sales world, if you're not disciplined, you'll get blown wherever the winds take you. Tom Ferry told me, "Whether it's taking 100 percent responsibility for the love and joy in my relationship, or building the business that I've built and having as many clients as I have, it's all about responsibility. Discipline and responsibility must be in alignment." If you want to be successful, you have to be disciplined. There's no other way.

Best Practice: The By Noon Effect

In sales, your output (activity) is largely self-managed. If you report to someone, your sales leader likely requires some form of call report so he or she can see what calls you made, what one-on-one meetings you conducted, what handwritten notes you sent, and so on. Sadly, for the majority in the sales industry, these reports are largely bloated with fictitious activity and seldom reviewed or challenged by sales management. Everyone knows it. Consequently, the salesperson is largely alone in a world of exaggerated activity. More often than not, this practice leads to poor results and periodic company or career changes.

Sales pros take a different approach. Having learned what is necessary to succeed, they use discipline to line up critical activities to be knocked down first. I refer to this as The By Noon Effect. The disciplined sales pro gets these non-negotiable activities done by noon, leaving the rest of the day to react and respond. Let's walk through the different elements of this proven process.

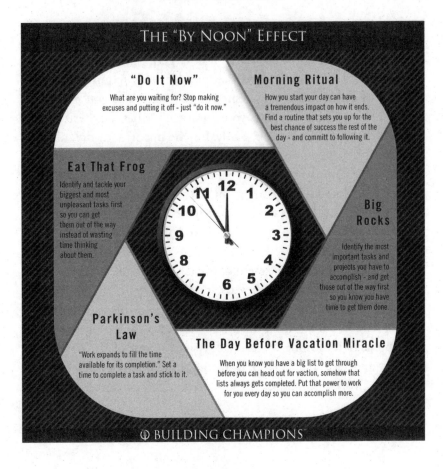

The "By Noon" Effect

"Do It Now"
What are you waiting for? Stop making excuses and putting it off - just "do it now."

Morning Ritual
How you start your day can have a tremendous impact on how it ends. Find a routine that sets you up for the best chance of success the rest of the day - and committ to following it.

Eat That Frog
Identify and tackle your biggest and most unpleasant tasks first so you can get them out of the way instead of wasting time thinking about them.

Big Rocks
Identify the most important tasks and projects you have to accomplish - and get those out of the way first so you know you have time to get them done.

Parkinson's Law
"Work expands to fill the time available for its completion." Set a time to complete a task and stick to it.

The Day Before Vacation Miracle
When you know you have a big list to get through before you can head out for vaction, somehow that lists always gets completed. Put that power to work for you every day so you can accomplish more.

BUILDING CHAMPIONS

Start with a Morning Routine

Productivity experts will tell you that the best way to be successful day after day is to stick to a routine. Humans are creatures of habit, and the more you do the important things, the easier it is to keep doing them. The By Noon Effect starts with a morning routine. Every successful sales professional I know has one. It's like a signal to your brain that lets it know it's time to begin.

The morning ritual can be simple. You could start with a quiet time of reflection or prayer. You could read a little from a book that motivates you. You may want to journal for a few minutes to get your thoughts in order. Then you might exercise, eat a healthy breakfast, and make time to talk with your kids or spouse. Whatever you decide to do, make sure it's a positive time that sets your day up for success. Then repeat it every day at the same time.

Get into the discipline of the routine. How you start your day can have a tremendous impact on how it ends. Find a routine that sets you up for the best chance of success the rest of the day—and commit to following it.

Establish Your Big Rocks

The first best-practice discipline is called Time Blocking. You can use it to identify your non-negotiable activities, the things that move the needle on your results, regardless of what else happens around them. Holly Reed told me, "The most important thing you do every day is your income-producing activity. That means you're actually talking to people, reaching out to people, face-to-face, phone-to-phone. That's the priority." Decide what your first things are and schedule them into your calendar. Stephen Covey calls this "putting the big rocks in first."

For the sales team leader, that might mean scheduling time with each salesperson to 1) review goals, 2) review activities, and 3) review sales results and help them identify where gaps exist. The discipline to set that time aside and commit to it is a key element in effective sales leadership. With sales leaders I coach, it is easy to get pulled into the reactive (and often addicting) problem-solving that frequently starts with,

"Boss, have you got a minute?" (Watch how often this happens to you now that I've called it out.) While availability to the team is important, committing to the discipline of sharpening the men and women on the front lines is critical. This is not an "either/or" proposition. It is, at best, a messy, fluid, and ever-changing focus on both. But it needs to be scheduled and protected. If you are a sales leader, being available to your sales team to answer questions and help solve problems can be handled in two ways: 1) empower people to start solving their own problems by having them research possible solutions before coming to you, and 2) have set hours when you are available for this purpose. (Many sales leaders will push back on this, lamenting that "my people need me," but is it possible that you're addicted to the firefighting? I see this *a lot*.) As Dr. Phil is fond of saying, "We teach people how to treat us."

Have you ever seen the sign that says, "Failure to prepare on your part does not constitute an emergency on my part?" Too many salespeople spin their wheels reacting to other people's problems while failing to tackle their own. Disciplined people identify and complete the most important tasks and projects first. This is non-negotiable and accomplishes two things. First, you always know that you've completed the work that matters. Second, it gives you a sense of accomplishment that carries you through the rest of your day. If you don't prioritize your time, you can be sure that someone else will do it for you.

The Day-Before-Vacation Miracle

The day before you go on vacation is an amazing day. It doesn't matter how long your list is or what is on your agenda.

Somehow you get it done. Your fingers dial the numbers and make the calls faster than you've ever done before. Gary Keller, author of *The One Thing*, calls this "the day-before-vacation miracle." He says that the only difference between the day before vacation and any other day is your discipline to plan your day and attack it with everything you've got. If you tackled every day with this same determination, you would get twice as much done in half the time.

An easy way to get started is to make a list at the end of the day of the most important things you need to accomplish the next day. It doesn't have to be complex. It can be a project or task you didn't finish or an entirely new thing. Creating a list at night gives your subconscious time to attack the problem overnight. It also enables you to hit the ground running the next day. You won't waste time deciding what to do—you'll do what you've already determined is important and likely in half the time.

Remember Parkinson's Law

Work always seems to expand to fill the time allowed for its completion. This is called Parkinson's Law. You can use this to your advantage. There's something about a deadline that can cause the biggest procrastinator to kick it into high gear. Once you've identified your non-negotiable items for the day, set a time to complete your tasks and stick to it. This may mean that you have to block out the time on your calendar and let other people know what you will be doing so they don't bother you.

I have a writer friend who realized that he did his best work from about 8:30 a.m. to 12:30 p.m., but he was wasting those hours responding to emails or attending meetings that were important to someone else. He could write in the afternoon and get his work done, but it took longer and required more editing. So he blocked out those four hours in the morning for his writing. He let everyone know that he wouldn't be checking email until after lunch. He scheduled any meetings for the afternoons. He silenced his phone and got to work. By setting deadlines and challenging himself to get his work done in that set time period, he accomplished his best work—each day by noon.

Worst First

Mark Twain said, "Eat a live frog in the morning and nothing worse will happen to you the rest of the day." How much time do you spend worrying about the difficult tasks you have to face in a day before you pull the trigger and just do them? It's hard to gauge the effect that worry has on your productivity, but we all know that it does. Worrying about a difficult sales call or a customer who has left you for the competition or a meeting with the boss seldom leads to anything good. And most of the time, what we worry about never happens anyway. My mother-in-law used to tell us to "not borrow trouble," loosely based on "Do not worry about tomorrow, for tomorrow will worry about itself. Let the day's own trouble be sufficient for the day." (Matthew 6:34)

White Collar Warriors know this truth: tackling the most difficult thing on their list first thing sets the tone for the rest of their day. So what "frogs" do you have on your list right now, and how long have you been putting them off? How much better will you feel when you finally tackle that challenge and get the difficult task done? Maybe you have to make a big sales call tomorrow and you are dreading it. You decide you'll just do it later in the day, and so you keep kicking the can down the road, worrying about something that you could just knock out and be done with. If you're an "eat the frog" kind of person, you harness that discipline, pick up the phone, and get the call over with.

In his book *The 4-Hour Workweek*, Tim Ferriss writes, "What we fear doing most is usually what we most need to do. Resolve to do one thing every day that you fear." I will add that you need to do that difficult thing early. Knock it out, and you'll feel confidence born of accomplishment. I keep a baseball-sized frog made of onyx on my desk to remind me of this every day. I often give coaching clients an action plan: buy a frog. I want them to put a frog—stuffed, crystal, onyx, or brass—on their desk to remind them of this important concept. If you have the discipline to do the worst thing first, you set up the rest of your day for success. That call you don't want to make, the expense report hanging over your head— knock it out first, and the rest of the day will be easier—and you'll feel better for having done it.

Do It Now

Can I be brutally honest with you? You already know what you should be doing today. It's not a mystery. If you want to be a successful salesperson, you have to make calls and ask for the sale. If you want to lose weight, you need to eat fewer calories and exercise more. If you want to accumulate wealth, you need to spend less than you earn and invest. Entrepreneur Derek Sivers puts it succinctly: "If more info were the answer, we'd all be billionaires with perfect abs."

Knowledge is not the problem; discipline is. You know what to do. If you want to be a success, you have to take action. Stop waiting, get rid of your excuses, and just do it now.

The Power of Flow

Larry Kendall is one of the founding partners of The Group Inc. Real Estate in Fort Collins, Colorado. The Group is one of the most productive real estate companies in the country. In his book, *Ninja Selling*, he describes his version of flow as being the ongoing follow-up with prospects. It is both automated and live. According to Larry, "Flow fixes everything." I couldn't agree more. The discipline to stay in touch leads the sales pro over time to the contracts, signatures, and acknowledgements that he or she needs to post stellar results.

Larry has been in this business for forty-five years and has over 200 agents, whom he calls Ninjas. He's developed a system in which disciplined action over time—making phone calls, sending handwritten notes, emailing clients and prospects, sending postcards, and having ongoing contact with prospects—creates predictably consistent results. What separates Larry's success from that of most others is his dedication to flow. Most people agree that constant contact and follow-up are important, but they do it only when they think about it. *When they think about it*—I'm calling this out because it's a killer of productivity. Larry has made flow a part of his organization's culture. When he teaches flow, he's saying you have to build it into your system.

He automates flow. If you want to add the power of flow into your routine, first determine which contacts you need to cultivate. Then set automatic reminders on your calendar at regular intervals. You have the technology, so make it work for you. When the reminders pop up, don't ignore them. Don't hit snooze and go back to whatever else you think is important. *This* is important! Follow up with these prospects like your life depends on it. Repeated disciplines over time will produce exceptional results. Trust the process; the results will take care of themselves.

Lumpy Cash Flow

One of the best benefits of harnessing the power of flow is smoothing the peaks and valleys of your sales results. In sales, it's not uncommon to think month-to-month. Often sales-people will engage in a flurry of activity—market, market, market, call prospects, make appointments, and send notes. Soon they start to get a lift. But then they stop marketing in order to close those deals and, inevitably, their business falls off. Then the cycle repeats itself. This never-ending cycle of up and down is stressful and ineffective. One entrepreneur calls it having "lumpy cash flow."

This up-and-down routine is common for most sales professionals when they don't keep prospects in the pipeline. When the pipeline runs dry, they start to panic. Because they weren't disciplined with flow, the cycle resets. When I coach salespeople to help get them out of this cycle, I focus on three things: routine, systems, and team. To become consistently successful rather than reactionary, all three components must be in place.

First, develop a routine. A routine is just a simple way to go about your day. When you develop a morning routine, you are telling your brain it's time to begin and what you want it to do every day like clockwork.

Second, develop systems. Systems work within your natural tendencies and inclinations. They work *with* you rather than *against* you. When you arrive at home, you probably have a place where you put your coat, your purse or wallet, and your keys. It's probably someplace that's close to the door so you can easily grab and go. Imagine how difficult it would be if every time you came home, you had to decide where to hang up your coat or place your keys. What a waste of time—and the next day you'd be frantically looking for your keys. Instead, your system has become a habit. You probably don't even think about it. Your muscle memory takes over.

You can create systems like this for selling as well. Disciplined sales professionals have systems that work for their industry and customers. They know their clients, and they have a specific system in place for meeting their needs. When you create a system, you no longer have to think about what you need to do—it becomes routine. Just like any habit, it will seem strange at first. But as it becomes second nature and keeps the pipeline full, with optimal flow, you'll start seeing results.

Charles Duhigg describes the power of habits: "Habits, scientists say, emerge because the brain is constantly looking for ways to save effort."

When you build habits and systems, you can stay focused on your rainmakers and referral relationships that generate most of your leads. Do this with enough consistency and you will establish top-tier customers and productive relationships that require only minimal effort to maintain and produce maximum results.

Third, develop a team. I'll unpack this more in chapter nine, but know that just like military leaders have a hierarchy in place in which every servicemember does his or her part, a disciplined sales professional works closely with a team. Strong teams work together to bring out the best in one another. You may be the frontline person who interacts with the customer, but your entire team is vital for making the customer happy.

You maximize results when you keep one eye on the customer and the other on your team.

Earn the Cigar

The best of the best march through pain and rejection to make contacts, have conversations, put on or attend events, and build a solid follow-up plan that generates success. It's not flashy or sexy, but grinding it out day after day separates the merely adequate from the exceptional. Most of us have a tendency to want to celebrate before a celebration is in order. In my experience, people often reward themselves before they actually do the work. Our society is kind of geared that way. But disciplined people who take ownership of their success behave differently. They earn the cigar.

Here's what I mean by that. When I start coaching a client, I often ask about weekly and daily routines. A new client once told me he visited a cigar shop several days a week at three o'clock in the afternoon. I sensed a problem and said, "You didn't tell me you owned a cigar shop."

"Oh, I don't own a cigar shop," he replied. "I just go to the cigar shop."

I asked him if he was getting a lot of business out of his visits there. He told me he didn't think he'd ever gotten any business out of it. I gently lowered the boom: "So on the one hand, you're telling me you want to increase your business by 50 percent, but three days a week you're going to the cigar shop, at three o'clock in the afternoon. How's that working out for you?"

There was silence on the other end of the line. Then he cleared his throat and said, "It's not working at all." So I asked him to take out a pen and paper and write down these five words: *I didn't earn the cigar.* I had him repeat the words back to me. *I didn't earn the cigar.*

Our brains are wired for reward, and that's something you can use to your benefit. You associate cigars with celebrations of a birth, signing a deal, or launching something new. In other words, you light up your cigar *after* you've done something worth celebrating, not before.

This client was buying three cigars a week while underperforming. He was training his brain to accept the celebration before he had done any of the hard work. So we developed a plan of intentional activity to fill his pipeline back up. Over the next few weeks and months, he got into a disciplined rhythm. He stopped leaving early and visiting the cigar shop. He set small sales goals, and when he achieved them, *then* he would get his cigar. Today, his production is *dramatically* higher, and he enjoys his cigars at the appropriate moments. Sweet.

Earning the cigar is difficult. If you want to rise above ordinary, you have to be disciplined. Earn the cigar and then celebrate. I promise it will be worth it.

Discipline Plus Integrity

As a coach, one of the things I look for is if a client has already learned discipline at a younger age—through sports, martial arts, music, academics, or the military. I see this a lot in the military elite I interview. Most of them entered the military with discipline already part of their lives from other areas, such as athletics (Navy recruiters actually scout water polo players as potential SEAL candidates). What circumstances have you already overcome in life by being disciplined? Think about the goals you've set and how you achieved them. Where did you learn discipline in your life? Did an adult model discipline for you? Sometimes to overcome a current struggle, you have to remember how you overcame a previous struggle.

I can tell you that I did not learn discipline at a young age, and learning it as an adult (like learning a new language, or I guess pretty much anything) is much more difficult. If someone brings discipline into the coaching relationship, our job will be much easier. If we have to hone that over time through accountability, it is a much more difficult process— not impossible, just more work.

If I just described you, know that I was describing myself not that many years ago as well. Know that if your *why* is big enough, the *how* will develop. The key to developing discipline is to recognize that it is going to take time. Anything worthwhile does. Successful people, no matter what their field, recognize that they are going to get knocked down. But every time they get knocked down and stand back up, they are stronger. Every time they attack a problem with discipline, they improve. Discipline keeps you from quitting, and in my experience, that is the most important element of success.

Discipline is also tied to integrity. Holly Reed told me, "Discipline requires us to be consistent; we have to be mindful of our words, we have to know what we're promising, we have to mean what we say and live out what we tell others we are going to do." What do you do when no one is watching? Disciplined people have the integrity to do what is right all the time, not just when someone is looking over their shoulder. This means that you are driven to push beyond your discomfort and do the difficult work before you. You don't stop, because you have an inner drive that's based on your integrity. You refuse to cut corners, and you are unwilling to do anything that jeopardizes your mission. As Lieutenant General Wooley told me, "Discipline is the thing that keeps you from succumbing to that temptation of knowing that you'll never get caught, nobody will ever figure it out."

A salesperson is under constant pressure to succeed, perhaps more than most other occupations. And the numbers tell the story. Either you are producing or you're not. The temptation to cut corners can be immense, but the better option is to develop a routine and establish discipline that keeps your pipeline full. Play the long game and form relationships with customers that withstand the ups and downs that are inevitable in business. Feed and water those relationships, and they will take care of you. This simple truth alone can be a game-changer for the sales pro. Overcome adversity by sheer, dogged persistence. Earn the cigar. Set small goals that lead to big outcomes over time, and when you succeed, celebrate.

Do the thing that you know you need to do—*the next right thing*. That's it. What's the next right thing for you? You know what it is, but you need to engage the discipline to do it. Your success hinges upon your next step. Where will yours take you?

Closing the Gap

The following section provides some questions that will help you assess your current level of discipline, apply some of the tools you've learned in this chapter, and maintain what you've learned as you establish new disciplines that become habits.

Assess

- If you had to grade your overall discipline level on a scale of one to ten, what grade would it get? Do your personal disciplines and business disciplines balance out, or are you more disciplined in one area?

1 2 3 4 5 6 7 8 9 10
(circle one)

- What experiences in your life have helped you establish discipline? How can you take what you've learned through other pursuits and use it to be more disciplined in your sales routine?

_____

_____

_____

_____

_____

- What is your reaction to The By Noon Effect? Have you ever considered when you are most productive and set a plan in place to maximize that time? Which area or areas do you need to add to your daily routine to maximize your mornings?

_____

_____

_____

_____

_____

Apply

• Sometimes you can get bogged down in the day-to-day and lose sight of the goal. What is the worst-case scenario for you if you aren't disciplined? What's the best-case scenario if you are disciplined and succeed? Once you've established your range, implement a system to keep yourself on track.

_____

_____

_____

_____

• What is the next right thing that you need to do to become more disciplined? Make it a priority to do that thing each day for the next two weeks. Keep track of when you did it and what the results were.

_____

_____

_____

_____

Maintain

- See the example of the discipline tracker at WhiteCollar WarriorBook.com. Use it to identify three non-negotiable disciplines that you must do each day to be successful. Fill these in for the week and make them your priority. Don't tackle any other projects until you've done these three items.

_____

_____

_____

CHAPTER 5

FEAR

Lesson 3: Your Fear Must Become Your Friend

"Inaction breeds doubt and fear. Action breeds confidence and courage. If you want to conquer fear, do not sit home and think about it. Go out and get busy."

—*Dale Carnegie*

Army Ranger Captain Chad Fleming (retired) has faced fear head on. He did not emerge from battle unscathed, but he walked out on the other side under his own power. Early in his first deployment to Iraq, he found himself embroiled in a fierce battle for his life. Ironically, he had only eighteen hours to go when his commanding officer gave him one last mission. A high-profile target had been located, and Chad's unit had been tasked with going after him.

After an unsuccessful daytime patrol, the convoy found themselves low on fuel. As they took cover under a bridge, they began taking small-arms fire. That attack quickly escalated into a barrage of grenades. One grenade landed two feet behind Chad. Another landed in front of him. The combined explosions nearly took off his left leg below the knee. As he scrambled to reach safety on the roof of his vehicle, a round pierced his thigh and knocked him to the ground. Here's how he described the harrowing scene to me:

> *When the grenade detonated one foot away from me and I sustained major damage to my leg, my only thought was, "Am I going to die?"* **In that moment, my training kicked in.** *I realized that me shutting down could not only be the death of me, but everyone else as well. Right after that happened, the second grenade detonated. I was shot when I got out of the Humvee and had now been blown up twice. I used my belt as a tourniquet and my rifle as a cane.*

Incredibly, Chad relied on his training to keep himself alive and continue fighting until he lost consciousness and woke up in a field hospital with a badly damaged leg. He would face more than twenty surgeries over the next twenty-six months before he made the ultimate decision to have his leg amputated. According to Chad, his decision to amputate his leg had nothing to do with his own discomfort; he wanted to lead men into battle without slowing them down.

On that day in October 2005, Chad Fleming faced his fears. Wounded in battle, he overcame those fears. After six deployments, five of them with one leg missing, Captain Chad Fleming had earned two Bronze Stars and three Purple Hearts. It's safe to say he knows a thing or two about fear:

*The physical result of fear is a shutdown of all comfort zones. Vision narrows, the heart races, and you lose all rational thought processes. You have to channel and focus. Lives depend on your leadership in these moments. **Fear can be the ultimate smack in the face.***

Fear Is Different from Being Afraid

Former Navy SEAL Marcus Luttrell, author of *Lone Survivor*, once said, "Fear is a force that sharpens your senses. Being afraid is a state of paralysis in which you can't do anything." Everyone faces fear at some point in life. Fear is a byproduct of living. It comes as a result of recognizing how small you are in the grand scheme of things. But fear doesn't have to paralyze you. In fact, warriors recognize that experiencing fear is very different than being afraid. When you recognize the difference, you realize that fear can be a catalyst that brings out your best. It stimulates you to do more and be more than you ever thought you could.

Being afraid is paralyzing. It makes you focus on the size of the problem rather than the effectiveness of your training or the inner strength you possess. The truth is that no matter how afraid you are of your circumstances, there is always something you can do. Those circumstances will eventually pass. Overcoming fear then becomes a mindset you adopt. This mindset helps you make fear your friend.

The Effects of Fear

If you've lived long enough, you've felt the effects of fear. Physically, fear can shut you down and cause you to freeze. It can make you physically sick and unable to move. Mentally, it can paralyze you. It stuns you, and since you can't figure out what to do, you don't do anything. You freeze, and in that moment your fear takes over and you've lost the battle.

Recently, when I was working with the Boot Campaign, I had a conversation with a severely wounded Army sergeant. He told me that he'd hit the ground, newly deployed in Afghanistan, fired up and ready to take on the Taliban. But as soon as the air-raid siren went off at the forward operating base, he felt a chill across his chest. He was appropriately trained, but fear unexpectedly gripped him physiologically.

But fear can also attack you in situations that aren't life-or-death, and its effects can be just as devastating. Just like a warrior's fear may cause hesitance to act in a crisis, a salesperson's fear may cause that same reluctance to move forward. The term is "call reluctance," and it refers to a salesperson's tendency to do anything other than make sales calls. In their book *The Psychology of Sales Call Reluctance*, George W. Dudley and Shannon L. Goodson write that "sales call reluctance consists of all the thoughts, feelings, and 'avoidance' behaviors that conspire to keep otherwise talented, motivated, potential high-level salespeople from ever earning what they're worth."

Perhaps you can relate. Maybe you've dealt with the struggle too. You may not admit it to anyone but yourself, but selling can be a scary business. No one likes to be rejected, and each time you hear *no* it feels like a personal affront to your abilities. So you do everything you can to *not* make the call. You make call lists of potential customers; you check inventory levels, shipping schedules, mortgage rates, or the latest trends in sales and marketing. You stay busy, but you don't produce.

When I first went to work for Century 21, I had been in the office for a week and one day I was sitting there with my briefcase at my desk. My boss walked over to me and said, "What are you doing?" I said, "Well, I'm getting ready to get organized, you know, to get my ducks in a row and start making some calls."

He looked down at me with a mix of exasperation and understanding, and I'll never forget what happened next. He picked up my briefcase with papers sticking out of it—a nice Hartmann leather briefcase, by the way—and he opened the window and slung it out into the parking lot. As it sailed through the air and landed with a thump, he said, "The business is out there."

Welcome to Sales 101.

He then proceeded to rip into me and said, "I've been watching you this week, and you've just been working on your 'busy kit.'" Basically, he pointed out that I'd just been busy doing nothing. I'd spent a week *thinking* about selling without making the first call to a prospect or customer. I'd cost the company money without bringing in anything to contribute to the bottom line.

I've never forgotten that lesson. My fears—of rejection, of coming across as pushy, of asking for the sale—had paralyzed me. I'd created a busy kit and moved papers around, brainstormed a plan, and thought about how I would sell when I began selling, but I *hadn't done the work*. I believe any salesperson can identify with this because—while rewarding—selling can be incredibly uncomfortable work.

Prospecting Is Emotionally Uncomfortable

The fear of producing (in this case asking for the sale) parallels something to which any creative person can relate. Author Steven Pressfield, in his book *The War of Art*, refers to this battle as the Resistance. He says the Resistance is that invisible foe that we all face when we try to do anything worthwhile. The Resistance is anything that requires you to get up early, work hard, make wise choices, face your fears, and push on through adversity. To each person, the Resistance looks and feels a little different, but make no mistake—we all face it.

Salespeople in particular face Resistance because, at its core, prospecting for sales is emotionally uncomfortable. You are calling people you may not know. You are asking them to trust you enough to exchange their hard-earned dollars for your goods or services. You are approaching them with what you consider a fair price and hoping they agree. All the while, that small voice in the back of your mind is whispering to you that you aren't good enough, that they are going to say no, that people will think you are a fraud. And so the fear kicks in and takes hold.

So what do you do? A tried-and-true trick is to procrastinate. I did that my first week at Century 21. I'm sure you've done it too. You look busy doing sales-y things, but you don't ask for the sale. Pressfield says this:

> *Procrastination is the most common manifestation of Resistance because it's easiest to rationalize. We don't tell ourselves, "I'm*

never going to write my symphony." Instead we say, "I'm going to write my symphony; I'm just going to start tomorrow."

US Army colonel Bob Hart (retired) told me how dangerous the fear that leads to paralysis can be:

> *The worst thing to do is to fail to react at all out of fear—it is better to make the wrong decision and do something than to do nothing at all and lose control and momentum in your environment. I have seen this more often in the professional world, not in combat, where people try to mitigate risk so much in order to avoid failure that they fail to move at all or do so in such an inefficient manner that their organization and team are hobbled and unable to optimize their performance and never succeed.*

Can you relate? Have you let fear get the best of you and allowed the Resistance to worm its way into your mind? Has tomorrow become your default start date? If so, there are ways to kick the Resistance to the curb and take back control of your fears. They've worked for the clients I've coached, and they'll work for you too.

Approach Sales with the Right Mindset

If you want to overcome your fear of selling and make fear your friend, you have to start by changing your mind. The first step to doing that is to recognize that you won't make every sale. No matter how good of a salesperson you are, sometimes *you won't get the sale*. You may not mesh with some customers. Your product or service may not meet their needs. You won't be able to deliver in the right time frame. There are countless other variables that may happen to prevent you from getting the sale. It's important to remember that it's OK. Every no may actually get you closer to a yes.

Another way to change your mindset is to play the long game. What if instead of trying to secure a single transaction that resulted in a commision, you built a relationship that resulted in a steady stream of commissions? When that becomes your aim, it lessens the fear that comes as a result of a possible no. You begin to see the possibility of having conversations rather than reciting a sales script. Remember, a no today is not a bad thing if it leads to an enlightening conversation and a better understanding of a customer's future needs. Pay attention, write down what you learn, and file it away for the next call. Remember the importance of flow. You can't develop flow when you make contact with a customer only once.

The last way to change your mindset is to know when to stop. Some of your fears may come from worries that you will come across as too pushy. It's one of the oldest sales stereotypes around. I do a lot of coaching in the mortgage industry. In that industry, people often say, "I'm a mortgage professional," but not, "I'm a salesperson." Why? People often associate salespeople with used-car salesmen. They picture slimy guys with fake smiles, wearing blue suede shoes and shiny suits, saying with a wink, "What's it gonna take to put you in this car today?"

Deep down, your fears may make you feel like you are that person. But the truth is, you can be a good salesperson without being slimy. Holly Reed says she quickly discovered that your motives often make all the difference. She told me, "If your motive is to get out there and find the people who need you, and you're not using manipulation, then go into that knowing that you have good motives. Yes, it's scary because it's something new. But if you know your motives are right, and you're just talking to them about how you can be a service and help them, fear diminishes." Be conversational and try to get to the root of customers' needs. Become a confidant who is in their corner, not a salesperson just trying to make a buck. When you learn to view yourself as a valuable part of their success, it will neutralize your fear and unlock your value.

Strategies to Overcome Fear

It sounds a bit ironic, but to conquer fear, you cannot be afraid of fear. Most people wrongly perceive fear as the enemy. Fear is an emotion, just like anger or sadness or joy. It has the power to influence us only if we give it that power. So the question you need to ask is, "What is the positive side of fear?" Chuck Swindoll says about attitude, "I am convinced that life is 10 percent what happens to me and 90 percent how I react to it." This same sentiment can apply to fear.

Will you be fearful at times? Of course. You're human. It's natural to be afraid. But what separates those who are paralyzed by fear from those who use fear to their advantage is how they react to it. When you recognize that fear will come, you neutralize its power over you.

In the military, if you aren't afraid, then something is wrong. In combat, military professionals face life-or-death situations that require an ability to mangage fear and use it to their advantage. Fear causes that extra-acute awareness, caution, and deliberate action taken in dangerous, uncertain, stressful circumstances. The postitive side of fear is that it sharpens you and primes you and makes you ready for action.

Prepare for Fear

So if you know fear is coming, there are ways to prepare for its arrival. For many military personnel, one of the scariest things they have to do is jump out of a perfectly good airplane and parachute to the ground. It's absurd to think that you'll get to that open door, wind rushing by at over one hundred miles per hour, and be completely without fear. You are going to be scared, and you will not want to jump.

Nick Palmisciano describes the process this way:

> *One thing the Army does incredibly well is breaking things down to simple steps. When you go to Airborne School, you learn things in a very simple sequence. When to stand up, when and how to hook up, how to check your buddy, how to clear your line, how to exit the plane, how long to count before pulling your reserve, how to check your chute after opening, and what to do if there are any issues. Then you train over and over and over again until you can do it all in your sleep.*
>
> *When you finally jump the first time, you are scared out of your mind, but you know many have done this before you; you know you have great training and great equipment. You do not want to miss a step.*

The fear sharpens you. It's a reminder that "this is for real now."

When you embrace that fear and remember that you've prepared for this, all of a sudden your training kicks in and your fear takes a back seat. This is why you've trained. So you go through the routine that you practiced on the ground. When you give your brain something else to focus on, in this case training, you can prepare for the fear that will inevitably come your way.

In sales, the same principles apply. You have to recognize ahead of time what you are going to encounter. Preparation takes the sting out of your fears. It tells your mind that you've got this, you won't be surprised, and you've planned ahead so that any objection that comes your way is one you can handle.

If you do this, plan ahead and be ready for what comes your way; your fears will lose their sting. You will not have the same level of fear or anxiety, but it won't go away entirely. But when you are prepared for it, it loosens its grip and doesn't scare you as much. Tom Ferry says it best: "Knowledge equals confidence and ignorance equals fear." The positive side of fear is that it allows you to be prepared. When you are prepared, you can conquer whatever comes your way. Fear is extremely useful when it goes hand in hand with training and hard work; but on its own, it simply paralyzes you into uselessness.

Allow Fear to Sharpen Your Vision

At its most basic level, fear kicks your adrenaline levels up and promotes the "fight or flight" mentality. If you were attacked on the street, the threat would be immediately clear. You wouldn't wait to see what would happen; you would either fight or run. There comes a time when you can't think or worry anymore—you just need to act. In this case, fear is a good thing because it can actually sharpen your vision. In these situations, everything else fades into the background, allowing you to focus on the danger at hand.

Nick Palmisciano says you have to push the fear back in order to amplify your focus. I like it. When you get a handle on your fears, you can use them like a searchlight to illuminate the areas you need to focus on. Inconsequential worries fall away, and what you need to do becomes crystal clear.

What's your vision for your sales goals? Are you clear on that vision, or have you allowed fear to cloud the way to your why? When I was sitting at my desk that first week at Century 21, I didn't have a sharp vision for what I needed to do. I allowed all of the other things I was doing to distract me from the issue at hand. When my boss chucked my briefcase out the door, it woke me up and made me realize that being fearful wouldn't help me earn the income I desired. It wouldn't help me reach the goals I had set for myself.

Once I realized this, my fear became an impediment, something that was in my way. It clarified my vision and gave me the stamina to push through and tackle the difficulties I faced. And once I started making those calls, my fear receded and my confidence grew.

Stay Alert, Bust Out of Ruts

Human beings are creatures of habit. We find what works and stick to it. Sometimes this is a good thing, as we discussed in chapter three. Thanks to habits, you don't have to relearn to tie your shoes each morning, figure out how to make coffee, or recall scripts you've made part of your routine.

But becoming too much of a creature of habit can put you in a rut from which you cannot escape. When the early settlers were moving westward across the United States frontier, they loaded up their belongings in Conestoga wagons. You've probably seen pictures of these wooden wagons with tall, narrow spoked wheels and white canvas tops. Pulled by teams of oxen, these wagons would stretch out along the prairie in a long line. As the wagon trains rolled westward, their wheels would carve ruts into the plains. Some of these ruts are still visible today. These ruts would deepen and provide a track of sorts that subsequent wagons would follow. This was great if you wanted to go where the ruts took you. But what if you wanted to go in a different direction?

Chances are, you've got some ruts in your sales routine. You may be afraid of what might happen if you tried to bust out of the ruts and go in a new direction. Maybe your company has always done things a certain way, but you think you've discovered a more efficient method. Or maybe you think you would face additional rejection if you forged a different path. You might even let a customer down or lose a customer altogether.

But what if those ruts are stopping you from becoming your best? What if they are actually handcuffing you and keeping you from better service, better sales, and better profits? White Collar Warriors aren't afraid to push boundaries and learn to get better. They push past the fear that says, "Yes, but…" and into the courage of, "Yes, and…." Managers will rarely fault you for trying something new in an effort to become better. Even if you fail, you learn something about yourself, your organization, and your customer. John C. Maxwell calls this "failing forward."

Stay alert and notice when you start to find yourself trapped in a rut. Pay special attention to when those ruts are caused by fear. These ruts can lull you into a false sense of security that ultimately can cause unintended consequences. Look for ways to get better every day. Make sure your customers know that you aren't happy with good enough—you are looking for excellent. They'll appreciate your candor and will likely do all they can to help you succeed, which in turn helps them succeed.

Discover the Worst-Case Scenario and Work Backward

I once had a friend who had a saying: "Work down from death." It sounds morbid, but he worked under the assumption that our worries were usually way worse than anything that actually happened. The fears that we face on a daily basis can cripple our effectiveness, so he came up with the Work Down from Death framework. He said that death was the worst thing that could happen. If you die, it's game over and you can't do anything about your problems. Next came an IRS audit. That's a painful and drawn-out process. From there, he would work backward until he came to his problem. Next to death, anything you face seems relatively benign.

Tim Ferriss calls this process Fear Casting. He realized that even if his worst fears came true, they weren't fatal, and he could bounce back from the effects of failure. It might take time and it might be a painful process, but he could emerge better on the other side. So when he is brainstorming new ideas that cause him fear or trepidation, he envisions the worst-case scenario first. Then he envisions the best-case scenario.

Although you can't predict the future, what actually will happen will fall somewhere between the two. Usually the end results fall closer to the best case than the worst case. Even if they don't, and you fall flat on your face, you've likely got a plan in place in the back of your mind to overcome your stumble.

What would it look like if you thought about the worst that could happen if you stumble? Would you lose an account? Would your commissions suffer? Would you lose your job? As terrible as these may seem, they aren't fatal. Accounts and commissions come and go. You probably won't be at that job forever anyway.

Now flip that thinking. What is the best that could happen if you make a gutsy choice and try something radically new? What if you landed your "never gonna happen in a million years" account? What if your commissions doubled? What if your leadership recognized your brilliance and asked you to teach it to the rest of the company?

Fear has a way of paralyzing us and keeping us from accessing our natural strengths and abilities. Don't let this happen! Trust your gut, realize you are better than you give yourself credit for, and take a chance. The results may just surprise you.

Tackle Your Fears Head-On

It's hard to imagine John Wayne ever being afraid of anything. He made his living portraying tough guys who always knew what to do and did it without batting an eye. Yet he said, "Courage is being scared to death, but saddling up anyway."

At some point we all have to face our fears and see what we're made of. Whether you are a child who has to peek under the bed to make sure the monster isn't there, a saleperson who has to pick up the phone and make a call you are dreading, or a soldier who has to put himself into harm's way, one day you'll have to face your fears. The funny thing is that once you finally face up to your fears and tackle them courageously, they don't look so big from the other side. You've grown, your fears have shrunk, and you are better for facing them with courage.

Hopefully you can get to this point sooner rather than later. When you get your mind in the right place and realize that you will always face fearful situations, but it's what you do in those situations that matters; you can "saddle up" and tackle those fears head-on. It may not be fun, but being able to look yourself in the eye and know you gave it your best is worth it.

How to Use Fear to Maximize Production

When you learn the strategies to help you overcome fear, the next step is to turn that fear from foe to friend. This is what separates the casual salesperson from the White Collar Warrior. Using fear to maximize your production doesn't have to be difficult. It starts with an attitude and finishes with instinct.

1) Shift Your Mindset

One of the biggest fears that a salesperson faces is the dreaded *no*. "No, your price is too high." "No, I already have a supplier." "No, I won't do business with your company." "No, we've always bought from your competitor." "No, you can't even speak to the person you need, because I'm the gatekeeper and I won't let you through." The list of nos can be endless!

And unfortunately, the dreaded no stops many salespeople before they ever get started. They dread the no so much that they never make the call.

The fear of rejection has killed innumerable budding sales careers. But the fear of rejection that stops you in your tracks can be overcome. It starts with a change in mindset. In sales, it has been said for years that you must learn to deal with rejection. "Thanks for the no" is an oft-quoted expression. It refers to the belief that sales is a numbers game, and every no brings you closer to a yes.

While I understand that thinking, I'd rather focus on the idea of *no* actually meaning *not yet*. It's a subtle shift, to be sure, but I've found that it can make all the difference. It's like the difference between *goodbye* and *see you later*. One sounds permanent, while the other is temporary.

There are so many sales professionals who simply didn't give up. I once signed up in a drawing for something free from a salesman named Lenny. I received whatever Lenny was handing out with no intention of ever buying anything. But part of Lenny's training was to follow up and realize *no* was really *not yet*. Lenny kept checking in on me periodically. Lenny had flow. He kept in touch. He would call, he would send emails, he would just stay in touch with me and keep his name in my view. He wasn't a pest even though I didn't respond to him for years. And then one day, I needed the service he provided. Who did I call? Lenny.

Now I joke with people I coach and tell them one of two things will happen: you're going to engage with that person eventually, or they're going to get a restraining order. But persistence makes the point—I will not stop until I capture your business. I will stay in touch, I will keep adding value, and one day I will *earn* your business. You can't be a rock in people's shoes, obviously, but you can find other ways to add value. Learn something personal about them, send them a note or a link to an article or a video relevant to them, or be there in their time of need. If you just keep dripping, over time a percentage is going to convert.

2) Establish a Process That Works

A salesperson's best friend is establishing a process that works. You see this now with online entreprenuers who sell you their product or service. What's the first thing they are after when you go their website? An email address. Why? Because it gives them direct access to you. By giving them your email address in exchange for something for free, you've essentially said, "I give you permission to sell me something later." There are entire books about the right sequence of emails with the right words that convert prospects into sales.

But what happens when you've allowed your fears to get the best of you and you've let relationships linger and become stagnant? When I coach clients, I circle back to this question: "What one thing, if executed daily, would have the biggest impact on your business?" Most of the time they say they don't do a good job keeping up with their clients. Their inter-action is hit-or-miss, and they don't have a process in place to keep them connected. Sometimes so much time has passed that they are embarrassed to even make the phone call. Again, they fear what the client might say, so they remain paralyzed.

A sales trainer developed a letter that they can use. It's called the "I Goofed" letter, and it basically makes you own up to your failure. You send it to clients, and it says that what is most important to you is building relationships with people like them. To that end, it lets them know that although you haven't done a great job with whatever it is, any contact they get from you or your team moving forward will be tangible evidence that you are putting them first.

It's humbling to send a letter like this, and it's meaningful to receive a letter like this. Best of all, it sort of sets the expectation that you will be following up with a phone call. That's very helpful for a salesperson who doesn't want to make the call cold. I'll have my clients send a letter, then make the call. Generally, they'll send twenty to fifty letters out one week and spend the next week following up on those letters. It's a process that builds flow, and guess what? It works.

The best part is that this process builds the discipline we talked about in the last chapter. When you send out those letters, you establish a call list, upon which you can follow up. It breaks down something insurmountable into something manageable. Once this process is in place, it becomes habit.

Maybe you don't need to send out an "I Goofed" letter. (Although I'd be surprised if there's not one customer who has fallen through the cracks.) But you do probably need to establish a similar process. A process simplifies your day, because it becomes routine. Follow the routine. Get results. It's as simple as that.

3) Commit to the Process

Creating a process goes a long way toward alleviating your fears. The beauty of the process is that it breaks down the complex into the simple. Say you've got a list of one thousand clients you want to call. That's complex. Break that down into fifty clients a week, and that's ten phone calls a day. That's simple and achievable.

The breakdown can occur when you fail to commit to the process or you try to micromanage the outcome. Remember the concept of flow. Building flow takes time. It won't happen overnight. Lenny stayed with the process for years in some cases before he saw results. But he was smart; he let go of the outcome and trusted the process.

I like to think of the phrase "Some will, some won't, so what?" This mindset really helps my clients release their attachment of the activity to the result. I'll often tell them that if they commit to the process, the results will take care of themselves. *Some will, some won't, so what?* When you adopt this mindset, you get the sense that if one person you talk with says no, it doesn't really matter, because that's a part of the larger effort that you're committed to right now. It frees you up to focus on the flow and minimize your fears.

One word of caution, though. Make sure you aren't wasting your process on a lead that won't pan out. I do a lot of coaching in the mortgage industry, and that happens a lot. Mortgage professionals will create a list of Realtors whose business they want to pursue. But if they haven't done any homework about how much volume the Realtor does, some of those leads will be dead ends. Maybe you are trying to build a relationship with a nice lady who sells three houses a year—she's not able to send you many leads. You may think she doesn't like you, but she really doesn't have any leads to send. She only sold three houses last year. She's a nice lady who shows up at the sales meetings, but she only dabbles in real estate. To avoid wasting time in cases like this, the first step is to make sure you are focusing on the right targets.

The next step focuses on how to target them. Expect to be ignored. I try to instill in my clients the idea that most prospects are going to blow you off. It's almost like a game to see how much you will take before you disappear. It's like they've learned somewhere in their sales school that lenders are going to come after them. If they don't respond, you'll go away. But when you commit to the process, you don't go away. Just stay in touch. It's subtle, but you have to *assume the relationship*. If you assume the relationship, you're going to approach them differently, and they are going to respond differently.

You know rejection is going to happen, but you're in it for the long haul. Once you know the prospect has potential, you keep pushing. *Some will, some won't, so what?* And so you commit to the process, knowing that the results will take care of themselves. The danger in staying connected to the outcome is that subconsciously, you'll start thinking what you're doing doesn't work. Before long, you'll get discouraged. White Collar Warriors let go of the outcome. They commit to the process, knowing the process works. Others have gone before you; walk in their footsteps.

4) Be Uniquely You

When I worked for Century 21, my boss had a habit of craning his neck a certain way when he was talking to a client or giving a presentation. I began to subconsciously do the same thing. I didn't even realize it until my wife was kind enough to point it out to me. I thought she was crazy until I saw a video of myself speaking. Sure enough, there it was. I was trying to emulate my boss and wasn't even aware of it.

For sixty-seven seasons, Vin Scully was the voice of the Los Angeles Dodgers baseball team. He began his career in 1950 and finally retired in 2016. Each year, Scully would call each of the 162 regular-season baseball games. When Joe Davis took over after Scully retired, he asked for Scully's advice. Scully said simply, "Be you. You don't need to be me, and you don't need to be like anybody else. The thing that's going to make you successful is to be you."

The best way to overcome your fear and make it your friend is to simply be yourself. You are one of a kind, and everything that makes you unique will make you the best in your field. Yet far too many people try to conform to someone else's view of what they should be. It's good to imitate the best qualities of others, especially if they are successful, but not at the expense of your identity.

Sometimes a company unintentionally creates unrealistic expectations, or what Greg Cagle calls a "success box." These expectations can make you feel that if you're going be successful in this company, you must look, talk, and act a certain way—even if that's not you. But when people try to change who they are, to conform to what they think is expected of them, they're no longer positioned to deliver their best. Since they're not bringing their best to the team, they're not bringing their best to the company. They feel frustrated and become expendable.

Don't be that salesperson. You don't need to conform. You need to be you. Conforming is going to bring you mediocrity. Find your uniqueness, whatever that is, and then sell like crazy using everything that makes you, you.

It can be liberating to understand that the fear you're experiencing may be due to trying to be something you are not. You may be thinking, *My boss wants to do things this way, and it doesn't feel normal, doesn't feel natural—it's not me.* It takes courage to be yourself, but being yourself is vital to overcoming that fear and getting out of the success box.

To conquer your fear about not fitting in, do what you need to do within the culture of your organization, of course, but find the chord that only you can play, the one that will set you apart. You might be the person who does public presentations really well. Maybe nobody else on your team is using video. Today, video is game-changing. Find the thing that makes you, you and lean into it.

If it seems to run contrary to what "successful people" in your company or organization do, have a conversation with your sales manager or the leaders if applicable. Be courageous and say, "This is how I think I'm wired." Let them know you think you can really succeed by doing things this way. Be careful to phrase it as you're taking ownership of your own growth. Make sure they understand that you aren't faulting the environment they've created but that you think you've found a way to excel by using your natural strengths and abilities.

For me, in the coaching world, it was using video. Nobody else on my team is really comfortable with it yet, but I've been doing it for six years now. The best part is that it has changed my brand; it has changed my receptivity. When I travel the country and meet people at seminars for the first time, they'll frequently say, "I feel like I know you." You don't have to buck the system, but you do need to find your differentiator that comes from being you. Find the thing that would really help to set you apart in an authentic way and boldly do that thing.

Closing the Gap

When you learn to see fear in the proper light, it ceases to be fearful. It becomes just another weapon in your arsenal, and it can propel you to reach greater heights than ever before. Nick Palmisciano believes fear isn't something to overcome; it is an essential catalyst to growth:

Fear in itself is never a healthy response. Fear alone equates to hesitation, and hesitation either gets you killed (in the military) or pushes you from opportunity. **Feeling fear, on the other hand, is essential.** *The fear of being unprepared and losing a soldier forces you to train harder. The fear of not being able to support your family keeps you fully engaged in an entrepreneurial venture. Fear is extremely useful when it is hand in hand with training and hard work. Without the latter, it simply paralyzes you into uselessness.*

Fear, then, isn't the enemy. It's a friend. Learning to work through your fear unlocks your potential and equips you to work calmly and courageously through the most difficult of circumstances. The greatest antidote for fear is action. Determine what you need to do, and do it. Push fear out of the way and get to work.

The following section provides some questions that will help you assess your current level of fear, apply some of the tools you've learned in this chapter, and maintain what you've learned as you overcome your fear and make it work for you.

Assess

- On a scale of 1 to 10, assess your current level of fear when it comes to selling.

1 2 3 4 5 6 7 8 9 10
(circle one)

- What comes to mind when you think of call reluctance? Have you ever experienced it, and if so, what did you do to overcome it?

  _____

  _____

  _____

  _____

  _____

- How would you define the difference between fear and being afraid? How have you used fear to your advantage?

  _____

  _____

  _____

  _____

  _____

APPLY

- What is something that you used to be afraid of but are not afraid of anymore? How did you overcome that fear? Are there any takeaways that you can apply to conquer the fears you are facing now?

  _____

  _____

_____

_____

_____

- Write down the best-case and worst-case scenarios if you charged forward and faced your fears head on. What would the likely outcome be? If the worst-case scenario happened, how could you bounce back?

_____

_____

_____

_____

Maintain

- As a salesperson, what is your strongest unique quality? How can you maximize that quality and use it going forward to become a more effective salesperson?

_____

_____

_____

_____

- Think about a time when you were scared but "saddled up" anyway, and the results were positive. What process did you use to get the positive outcome? Can you use it going forward in other instances?

_____

_____

_____

_____

_____

CHAPTER 6

PLANNING

Lesson 4: Your Sales
Plan Determines Your Success

*"A good plan violently executed now
is better than a perfect plan
executed next week."*

—*George Patton*

The desired outcome was simple. Thirteen letters. Three words. *Kill or capture.*

The term *high-value target* might as well have been made for an enemy like this. The United States military and intelligence agencies had spent over fifteen years and untold sums of money in the search. But now that they had found the target, SEAL Team 6 needed a rock-solid plan for the takedown. Enter Vice Admiral William McRaven, proponent of making your bed first thing in the morning and commander of the Joint Special Operations Command. He literally wrote the book on Special Operations warfare.

McRaven was tasked with planning the raid, code name Operation Neptune Spear, that would either kill or capture the most wanted man in the world—Osama bin Laden.

The team established a plan and got to work. Using satellite images, they built two mocked-up compounds, one on the east coast and one on the west coast. They were correct down to the finest details. The CIA established a safe house close by the target compound in Pakistan to watch the comings and goings of the inhabitants. A highly sophisticated drone flew overhead and around the compound to take real-time images and confirm that Osama bin Laden was hidden there. They had the best intel possible, but President Obama was told that there was only about a 50 percent chance it was actually the man who had brought the Twin Towers down on September 11.

On May 2, 2011, it was "go time." The conditions were right; it was a moonless night. In the dead of night, two specially designed helicopters carrying twenty-three SEALs, an interpreter, and a dog set out to kill or capture the world's most wanted man. A backup team of SEALs flew to a location ten minutes away from the compound. In spite of all the planning, they immediately had to adjust when they arrived at the target. One of the helicopters had to make a hard landing, which ruined the element of surprise. Instead of being able to rappel down to the roof of the building, they had to storm through gates and over walls.

Ultimately, all the planning paid off. Because they had practiced the process continuously in the mocked-up version of the compound, they knew what to expect. They were as comfortable there as they would have been in their own homes. As they cleared the rooms and wound upward, they encountered minimal resistance and ultimately killed Osama bin Laden in his bedroom. They quickly grabbed his body and as many hard drives and files as they could. They destroyed the damaged helicopter and took off for the U.S. airbase in Bagram, Afghanistan.

Years of intense and detailed planning had resulted in a successful forty-minute raid. There were no American casualties, and they achieved their objective. Their plan had ensured their mission's success.

The Vital Process

Whether planning is like second nature to you or you have to work diligently to make a plan, one thing is true—the planning process is vital to mission success. Without a solid plan of attack, you have zero chance of completing your mission—whether that mission is taking down the world's most notorious terrorist or capturing your biggest sale. You may stumble upon some success and get lucky, but luck isn't a strategy for long-term success.

Planning aligns your mind with your mission. Each member of SEAL Team 6 executed his part of the mission because it was lodged firmly in his mind. They practiced extensively and developed contingency plans in case they encountered problems. When things didn't go as planned—and they never do—they improvised and adapted to conditions on the ground based on their plan. Their eyes didn't waver from the objective even though the execution of the plan had to change.

Nick Palmisciano says:

> *I believe that the planning process aligns everyone's mind and ensures that everyone knows the general steps that must be executed to achieve success and what success looks like (the intent).*
>
> *When I have planned extensively with my subordinates, we have done exponentially better than when our planning has been lacking, regardless of whether things have gone as planned or have gone vastly different than was expected.*

The not-so-technical term is "mission planning," and every member of the team must be involved. Mission planning identifies a target and explores every contingency around that objective. They literally rebuilt that compound so that they would be intimately familiar with its layout. Then they pounded away at the disciplines necessary to achieve the objective.

They trained, they rehearsed, and they practiced. They felt what it was like to deploy from the helicopters—to fast-rope into the compound. They knew the location of every gate and door and had a plan for breaching each one. They knew the height of the walls and practiced clearing them. They entered the rooms wearing night-vision goggles. They planned for encountering civilians and noncombatants and established a course of action for how to deal with that with minimal casualties. They knew their *desired end result*, and they did everything they possibly could to set themselves up for success.

Mission planning for the White Collar Warrior looks different from the military application, and yet there are strong similarities. The White Collar Warrior must have a clear objective in mind. The White Collar Warrior must gather as much intelligence as possible to make informed decisions. The White Collar Warrior must practice and prepare before he or she can execute with discipline. And just like the warrior, the White Collar Warrior must debrief after a mission to see what worked, what didn't, and how to close the distance between the two.

David Rutherford, US Navy SEAL (retired), observes that the best at mission planning are those who "have had their asses handed to them." The same is true in sales. I think it's human nature to take the biggest lessons from things that cause the most pain. I remember my grandfather taking me to a Jerry Quarry fight. Quarry was a popular heavyweight boxer in the late 1960s and early 1970s who fought Muhammad Ali twice. To me, he was just some fighter duking it out with the other guy, but I remember my grandfather telling me of his own amateur boxing experiences in the 1920s. My grandfather's nose was large and crooked. He told me it was as a result of getting it broken repeatedly in fights because he wouldn't listen to his trainer about protecting his face with his left. As soon as he did, his nose stopped taking a beating.

A salesperson who has been set aside, dismissed, or worse—lost a sale to another—has been punched in the face. He or she has felt the pain of defeat. The best of the best learn and grow from these mistakes. Though this process is painful, it brings receptivity to other ideas. When you have failed, you will listen more carefully to the sales leader who can share ways to overcome objections, uncover needs, and move the sales process toward a successful outcome. Failure doesn't have to be final unless you refuse to learn from it and adapt. We'll unpack more of the value of failure in the next chapter.

Bob Hart, US Army Airborne Ranger flight surgeon, says this about the importance of planning:

> *Attention to detail is often the difference between tragic failure and overwhelming success. Overpreparation is far better than failing to plan for contingencies. Failure to plan is planning to fail.*
>
> *This does not mean a rigid plan, though. Flexibility with the capability to mitigate adverse conditions and circumstances is key to success. Flexibility comes from planning through and identifying viable contingencies, and identifying resources that you can utilize and leverage to get the job done. Nothing ever goes exactly according to plan, but that is where training and preparation come into play, as they provide one with the foundation to solve complex problems if the plan doesn't play out.*

The important thing is to develop a plan. In fact, it's vital to your success. It doesn't have to be a perfect plan; there's no such thing. But the more you can anticipate problems on the front end, the more you can overcome them successfully on the back end.

The Benefits of a Well-Defined Plan

1) Clearly Identifies Your Goals

You live in a world that is filled with noise. Every day you are bombarded with messages, emails, advertisements, news headlines, social media posts and reactions, and other things that command your attention. It can become more than a little frustrating to deal with it all. Although chaos is part of the process, the best of the best learn to cut through the noise and focus on what is truly important.

Clarity is the enemy of confusion, but a well-defined plan helps you to separate the trivial few from the vital many and establish goals that lead to your success. Think of a time when you've taken a road trip. Each mile marker along the way gave you information that helped you gauge your progress and stay on track. A well-defined plan is filled with options, outcomes, and adjustments to help you keep moving forward and tracking toward your goals.

2) Defines Successful Outcomes

What is your definition of *success*? If you don't know, then how will you know if you've achieved it? A well-defined plan defines successful outcomes. Yet so many people I have coached, especially in the sales world, simply show up, make some calls, and hope for success. This method involves a lot of turning around in circles and frustration.

The best warriors visualize success from the outset. It's why soldiers spend so much time practicing using their weapons. They know what the target looks like in their mind before they ever engage it in battle. Have you started to visualize success? What will it look like for you? A well-defined plan establishes the outcomes you need to be successful. It has components that are specific and measurable and easily tracked. Tom Ferry believes that visibility and measurement are vital: "If it matters, it's got to be measured. It's got to be visual. If you walk through my entire office, every goal is on display; it's visual and nobody can hide."

A well-defined plan helps you maintain optimism. It cuts through the mental clutter that stops you before you get started. It also helps you keep one eye on the long-term goals. Ferry says he tells his team, "I need you to spend 10 percent of your day, every day, on projects that are going to impact our team, our customers, and our universe in 2020." Building successful outcomes into your plan gives you targets along the way—build a call list of a specific number of prospects, make a specific number of calls a day, add two new pieces of business each week, or increase profits by 10 percent. Each target brings you closer to your goal, whether that goal's achievement date is next week or next year.

3) Outline the Steps for Success

One of Stephen Covey's seven habits for highly effective people in his book of the same name is, "Begin with the end in mind." Yet so few people create a plan for their days, let alone all the other areas of their life. Simply put, they drift. The starting point may be deciding where you want to finish, but it doesn't stop there. A well-defined plan outlines the steps for success. It is a road map and a visual reminder that when you do the things you've laid out, you will experience the results you desire.

In the military, a sniper works with a spotter. The two people rely on each other to successfully execute their mission. Firing a high-velocity bullet over vast distances requires precision and concentration. There are many factors trying to pull that bullet off its intended course. Moving the rifle an eighth of an inch could result in the bullet's being several feet off its mark. So the spotter looks at wind speed, distance to target, elevation, humidity levels, and countless other factors to give the sniper the best information possible for a successful outcome.

Your plan needs to look over all the outcomes and provide a process for navigating every obstacle you can uncover. You need a clear target and a well-thought-out plan to meet that target. Without a plan, it's like shooting an arrow blindly; if you don't know what you're aiming for, how will you know if you've hit it?

4) Identifies Viable Contingencies

The days of navigating through unfamiliar places have changed dramatically with smartphones. Instead of having to use a paper map, you can now type in an address, and using GPS, your phone will tell you which route to take, estimate your time of arrival, and warn you of hazards along the way.

The Waze app by Google has upped the game and taken navigation a step further. When you download this app to your phone, you become a "Wazer." You can essentially report on conditions as you are driving. If you see a road hazard, you can let other Wazers know. Ditto for traffic congestion, police, weather problems, and gas prices. Consequently, this app is a roadside community where real-time information constantly changes the plan. Using this constant updating of real-time information, the app adjusts your route and finds the shortest and easiest way to reach your destination.

The best plans are highly strategic but also incredibly flexible. Things often do not go as planned, so you have to adapt accordingly. Good plans mark out the best routes to reach the desired outcome but also provide redundancy and the ability to adapt as needed. If A happens, then you'll do B. If B happens, you'll do C. If B doesn't happen, then you'll do something else to get to C.

In an interview talking about the mission to kill or capture bin Laden, Admiral William McRaven said, "You always plan for the worst-case scenario, so we had a plan A and a plan B and a plan C and a plan D. Plan A went a little askew, so we immediately jumped into plan B, but we got our man." Of course, the SEAL Team 6 members didn't intend to crash their helicopter into the compound. But their plan was so well-devised that even that setback didn't jeopardize the mission. They simply regrouped, did what they needed to do, and kept moving forward.

5) Leverages Potential Resources

The Navy SEALs have a saying: two is one and one is none. This refers to building in redundancies and being prepared. The best plans leverage potential resources by planning for failure. Things will go wrong. What you think will happen may not actually happen. There are many variables in play, so it pays to be prepared. Former Navy SEAL Richard J. Machowicz refers to this as "advantage stacking." He says, "You want to stack so many of the advantages in your favor that when the order comes, when the opportunity presents itself, you can't help but win."

This is the power of multiplication versus addition. In sales, if you add one customer at a time, you will grow, but if you add customers who sing your praises and refer their friends and acquaintances to you, then you will multiply your growth. The multiplication process may start out more slowly, but in the end, it is explosive.

A very practical example of this is using the information you gather from one customer to help you close the sale with another customer. When you are playing the long game and building relationships with your customers, those relationships are often one of the best sources of your success. When you can string together information from multiple sources (a competitor's pricing from another customer, market conditions, supply levels, and the like) you can use it to paint a clearer picture of the landscape and make informed decisions going forward.

A Proven Plan for Staying on Mission

Several years ago, I began coaching a client named Josh Mettle. He was in the mortgage industry, and he really wanted to go after loans that were profitable and created a niche market for him. He had the spark of an idea to get there, so I just listened and asked him to spend some time thinking his idea through. We made a plan to talk again in a couple of weeks and create a plan of action.

Two weeks later, he called me back and explained that he wanted to focus on physician home loans. He explained that loans for physicians who've just graduated medical school and are moving into residency have historically been both unique and challenging to finance. This created an opportunity to serve an underserved market and disrupt the industry. It was a unique niche, and it intrigued me. When physicians enter residency, they often have to move to a different state. The upside earning potential may be huge, but residents need some help establishing their mortgage since it's based on future earnings, not present income.

Josh had this vision that he'd like to do more of these types of loans because no one else seemed to be exclusively focusing on them. So we used a One-Page Simple Business Plan created by Building Champions to get started. You can download a copy of the simple business plan at WhiteCollarWarriorBook.com.

Using this one-page document, we established his big overall theme. In Josh's case, it was physician home loans. He wrote that in a circle on the middle of the page in big, black letters. Next, we brainstormed the outcomes he hoped to achieve using the plan. Then we established the disciplines he would need to do every day to achieve those outcomes. Finally, we created a list of projects. These were small steps along the way, and each one had a target date for completion.

But the story gets better.

Since he was innovating a whole new niche, he hired a person from the medical device industry who knew the hospitals and doctors to be his liaison. When new physicians flew into town, he met them in a shiny black Escalade to pick them up. Josh and his team made lodging arrangements at a nice hotel. They made a plan to act as concierges and make the process as easy for the new physicians as possible. Unfortunately, this approach bombed. But from it, Josh learned some valuable lessons.

Josh was never one to give up, so what did he do? He wrote a book called *Why Physician Home Loans Fail*. Using what he learned from his initial missteps, he became known as the expert in physician home loans. Not just locally, but nationally. He touted it on his website and recorded videos in which he interviewed physicians. Now he's successfully closing physician home loans in all fifty states. In 2017, his team served over 650 physician families, and he has his sights set on serving 2,500 medical professional families by 2023. And it's because he has multiplied. He hired people underneath him, and he's built an organization in which he's got more people who know how to handle his inbound calls and opportunities. He's kept the flow going and is reaping the rewards.

Josh discovered a niche in which very few people were operating, and he maximized his role in that space. So just how did having a plan help him? I am certainly not trying to imply that his success is due to anything I did—Josh is a hustler, and he worked like crazy to establish himself. But I did help coach him to break his goal down into a manageable plan. And from there, he killed it. He used the one-page business plan, and now he dominates the market of physician home loans.

So what about you? Could a simple business plan help you turn your sales business on its head? By the way, the first step is treating your sales job like your own business. You have to own the process and not just show up and hope you stumble into some success. Make your business plan about *your business*. It doesn't matter if you are in direct marketing or if you are working for someone else. When you develop a business plan and take ownership of the process, you will succeed.

There are an awful lot of people in sales who don't think of their business as a business. But there's an ownership, an evolution that happens when you develop a business plan. It's simple and concise. For salespeople, it's very fundamental, and it's very easy to focus, and it's very easy to look at. If you print a one-page simple business plan out and put it somewhere where you'll see it every day, it focuses your attention. It's a reminder that says, "That's right. That's what I'm doing. All these crazy things are going on in my world, but I'm anchored to that one-page document that reminds me of my focus."

For many people, just the mention of creating a business plan causes anxiety. It may be happening to you right now. You may be thinking of a fat binder filled with market analyses, extensive plans for each phase of your growth, competitor information, branding and marketing info, and so on. Like many things in life, the worry is bigger than the problem ever could be. Because the idea causes so much anxiety, many business professionals never create a business plan, or if they do, they rarely use it. The result is a group of individuals who chase any opportunity that comes along and then drop it when it doesn't bring immediate results. As you can imagine, this is not the most successful way to run a business.

There is a better way. The solution is to use the simple one-page business plan that outlines what you will accomplish, where you need to make improvements, and what you will do to reach your goals. This simple document can often be completed in an afternoon, but the benefits are immense. This tool will guide you and your team while still allowing you the flexibility you need to adjust to changes in your market. Begin with your Theme or Focus. In the military, this is often referred to as "Commander's Intent."

We then focus on the three parts of the simple business plan and the steps you need to create yours.

1) Recon—Identify Your Desired Outcomes

You've likely heard the Chinese proverb, "A journey of a thousand miles begins with a single step." Ultimately, your business and your sales will never grow unless you move forward. Too many people are paralyzed by inaction because they perceive the road ahead to be too difficult. It can be daunting to consider every step along the way, so the simple business plan breaks the journey down into manageable pieces.

In the military, a scout goes out on reconnaissance missions to determine the lay of the land, the strength of the enemy, and the obstacles the team faces on the way to its objective. Having this advance information makes the whole outfit stronger. For your business plan, you need to start your recon process by identifying your outcomes. This is what you will measure. They may be in the areas of income, revenue, units, clients, or any other area in which you can quantify the outcomes you want. Once you know your outcomes, you can begin looking at strategies to reach them.

Another Chinese proverb is, "The best time to plant a tree was twenty years ago, while the second-best time is today." Stop talking about someday and get started now. The first step to growth is determining what it is you want to measure. What gets measured gets done. Determine what outcome, if maximized, will increase your growth, and make it a part of your plan.

2) Attack—Master the Necessary Disciplines

Discipline is often thought of as a dirty word, but the truth is that without discipline you will never reach the level of success that you desire (see chapter four). The important thing to remember in sales and in life is that changes happen incrementally. There aren't any overnight successes or failures. Rather, there are people who are consistently disciplined (or undisciplined), and each type faces the consequences.

General George S. Patton once said, "Nobody ever defended anything successfully; there's only attack and attack and attack some more." The disciplines section of the simple business plan teaches you to determine the actions you will take on a regular basis to reach your goals and attack them with fervor. It is important to ensure that your disciplines are clear, specific, and actionable. For example, "Talk to my loyal clients more" is not a discipline, but "Call five loyal clients each day" is.

Repeated discipline over time leads to improvement. Make it your objective to get 1 percent better each day. Compete with yourself to do better than the previous day, whatever that looks like in your business. Hold yourself accountable and track your progress. Specific, measurable goals that are realistic lead to positive results. You may not get there tomorrow, but you'll set yourself up for success.

3) Projects—Identify and Make Improvements

David Allen, author of *Getting Things Done: The Art of Stress-Free Productivity*, describes a project as "anything that is more than one physical action." Consequently, projects are not tasks or disciplines. They take a bit more time.

In the sales world, a project could be "Organize my database." This could consist of aggregating names and contact information from Outlook, a cell phone, and Excel into one Customer Relationship Management (CRM) system. It could also be setting aside training time to become proficient in a new software solution that will take time to master.

Author Michael Hyatt says the best way to get going on a project is to "launch and improve." Once you've identified your desired outcomes and mastered the regular disciplines, the next step is to monitor and adjust. You do this by creating project-based markers, or "gates" (like those a downhill skier maneuvers through), on the road to success. These projects are not ongoing disciplines; instead, they are one-time projects that, when complete, will enhance the way you do business.

By tackling manageable goals, you begin to change your thinking and your habits. Each success will bolster your confidence and move you closer toward your goals. As you undertake these projects, you'll learn how they connect you to the big picture of your plan and your goals. Be flexible, both in your thinking and your approach. When something works, make a note of it and do it more often. When it doesn't, note that too and set it aside. Now might not be the time, but it may be useful later.

Major Bob Hart recognizes the need for flexibility in planning:

> *Plans are always changing, even up to the minute before we leave, because we cannot control some of these variables. Flexibility and improvisation are often the keys to success. Mastery of the basics means we can apply our principles under any circumstance and still find success.*

It's important to remember that there's probably no plan in the sales world that is absolute. There just isn't. So the thing to do with your plan is to test, reassess, and re-evaluate. Maybe you are making calls, writing handwritten notes, sending emails, and you're not getting the results you want. Whatever it is, if you find that you're doing something that's not working, it's time to adjust. See what your returns are on that particular thing. If your methods aren't working, adjust. Make your calls at a different time of day. Use a different approach or purpose for the call. Give Slydial (voice broadcast) or Phone Burner (technology that allows you to make many more calls in a given time period) a try. In the case of email, try video email. As Tom Ferry says, "ABT—always be testing."

But just be careful. On the one hand, you have to give the process enough time to get traction to see if it's actually working or not; on the other hand, if it's clearly not producing results, then at a certain point, it's time to shift gears and do something different.

This mindset and willingness to adjust to circumstances on the ground are what soldiers have and do on each mission. The plan is vital, but when you actually get boots on the ground, you may have to adjust. You deploy with your plan, but then you encounter whatever you encounter. That's when you assess, adjust, and then redeploy. Assess, adjust, and redeploy as many times as it takes to meet your objective.

When you've completed your one-page simple business plan, this document will become your guide. It has the key information you need to stay focused on reaching your goals in the months ahead. For it to work, though, you must commit to reviewing the plan weekly and using it to guide how you invest your time and make decisions.

Old-School Tip

Having a plan is vitally important, but what good is the plan if you don't put it into action or if you refer to it only sporadically? My most successful clients have established a process for tracking their results. I'm a huge fan of old-school "thermometer" (or similar) tracking methods. You've probably seen the old United Way thermometers used for fundraising. They go outside on a billboard with a numerical goal. As the donations come in, the red line rises, indicating precisely how close the fundraisers are to reaching their goal.

I just saw a sign in the pro shop of a local country club; it was a board on an easel with a round dial and needle, and it was titled "Move the Needle." The club had about 300 members and a clear goal of 424 members. Since it was in everyone's best interest to add members, the club was very public about its goals and communicated those growth goals to its membership. This created buy-in for every person who saw that sign.

I have seen over and over again how White Collar Warriors can stay connected with their goals despite whatever interruptions, setbacks, or catastrophes unfold around them. The idea of having a simple, visual reminder of what's most important every day (calls made, notes sent, contracts written, and the like) will help you stay focused on the big picture and out of the weeds. Is it possible to use a digital approach to tracking your results? Of course, but personally I like the old-school way. It's an in-your-face approach to tackling your goals. It can't get lost in the digital world, and it's a bold declaration to anyone who walks by about what you intend to accomplish. It also serves to keep your team focused on where you're headed.

Closing the Planning Gap

For over fifteen years, the best and the brightest analytical and military minds searched for Osama bin Laden. They turned over every stone until they tracked him down. When they found out where he was hiding, they didn't rush in. They took their time. They gathered intelligence about his habits, his schedule, his routine, and his surroundings. They created a mock-up of his compound and rehearsed the take-down until it became second nature. They had backups and contingency plans should something go awry. When the time came to execute the mission, its success was a forgone conclusion, because they had planned for every eventuality. The only way it would have failed was if bin Laden somehow slipped away unnoticed.

Planning positions you for mission success. Whatever your mission is, it is doomed to fail without a plan. You may get lucky and stumble into some sales, or you may inherit someone else's accounts and hard work, but if you want to take ownership of your business and grow it to the next level, you must have a plan. The important thing is that you start. Move forward. Sketch out a plan. Launch and improve. An afternoon of work on your part may just transform your business and your life.

Assess

- The truth is that you never stay the same. You are either moving forward or regressing. How would establishing a plan help you move forward and reach your goals? What's stopping you from developing that plan?

  _____

  _____

  _____

  _____

  _____

- Think of a time when you tackled a project or mission that seemed overwhelming but you succeeded. How did having a plan in place help you break big objectives into smaller, manageable tasks?

  _____

  _____

  _____

  _____

  _____

- If someone asked you to describe your business or sales plan, how would you describe it? Could you easily articulate your process, or would you have difficulty?

  _____

_____

_____

_____

_____

Apply

- Start with your simple business plan. First, write down your theme in the center of a circle you draw on the page. It could be something thematic like "build the team" or "diversify." Regardless, it's for you and is designed to help you focus at the thirty-thousand-foot level as you engage in the daily disciplines at ground level. Next, determine your desired outcomes. They could be the amount you want to earn, a market-share goal, or something much more esoteric, like "Take Fridays off." Next, add primary disciplines. These are the key activities that you know will get you closer to your goals. Finally, write in the projects with specific end dates. These are the things that will take multiple steps to accomplish. (Dates drive disciplines.)

_____

_____

_____

_____

_____

Maintain

- Who do you have in your work life who keeps you accountable for your goals? Write the person's name below along with the ways you've benefited from that relationship. Best advice? Hire a coach.

———————————————————————————————

———————————————————————————————

———————————————————————————————

———————————————————————————————

———————————————————————————————

CHAPTER 7

FAILURE

Lesson 5: Your Failure Can Be a Gift for Growth

"Success is 99 percent failure."

—*Soichiro Honda*

David Berke was raised on the sound of screaming fighter jets screeching across the sky over his head. He lived in a Southern California town called El Toro with a Marine fighter base in his backyard. He told me, "At some point that got into my blood, and from watching them fly overhead at air shows, I decided that's what I wanted to do."

Berke graduated from flight school and eventually returned to Southern California to be stationed at Marine Corps air station El Toro. He was actually the last F/A-18 team pilot to launch out of El Toro before it was closed in 1998. After the attacks of September 11, he served seven months on an aircraft carrier flying missions to Afghanistan.

When he finished his tour, he was invited back to become a Top Gun instructor. Yes, *that* kind of Top Gun. He would agree to serve in Iraq and guide air strikes as a forward air controller in coordination with the teams on the ground during the Battle of Ramadi.

Throughout his stellar career, Berke learned valuable lessons about many of the things we've already discussed in this book. He has something very interesting to say about failure:

> *If you can embrace the fact that you will not be perfect, you will not achieve what you're looking for in the same manner of what's in your mind, failure becomes a tool to eventually [equip you] to be successful. We see these two like they're opposites. You're either successful or you're a failure. But if you fail and learn from that failure, collaborate with people around you, admit and own up to everything you did wrong, you will learn from that. Apply it and you will eventually succeed.*

In our conversation, Berke told me that he believes the real benefits of failure come when you hit rock bottom but don't stay there. By thinking of every single possible error you made, you can begin to take 100 percent ownership of those mistakes. You can then start to create solutions for those problems and let everyone see: "This is the way you do business, the way that your company does business, the way your team does business...you talk about everything you did wrong."

Rock Bottom

While I wouldn't wish it on anyone, it is amazing to me how beneficial failure can be for many sales professionals. Hitting rock bottom seems to light our fuses. It is relatively easy to ride on a wave when you haven't fallen off your board, been pummeled underwater by the washing machine churning of the water, and finally emerged coughing up salt water with snot coming out of your nose.

My wife, Toni, and I have a friend, a pastor and a surfer, who was hit in the eye with the front end of a surfboard several years ago and nearly lost his eyesight. It is still affected to this day. As a result, his awareness in the water is very different now. Failure has a way of making things look different.

Of course, failure is to be expected. It's part of the process of living. No one bats a thousand all the time. So if you can expect failure to come your way at some point, then you can also plan for it and prepare for it. Failure can define you, or it can energize you. You probably already have a certain amount of confidence, or you wouldn't be reading this book and trying to get better. Most failures you have faced were probably more of the situational variety. I see this often when coaching clients. They try something and it doesn't work, and so they need someone to help them navigate back out again.

For the White Collar Warrior, failure is more often than not a financial valley. I often hear, "I'm having a bad month." Perhaps you can relate. When bad months become strung together, you may have to sell assets to pay bills or borrow money from friends or family. It can be brutal. I know. I've been there.

My Own Rock-Bottom Moment

My own rock-bottom moment came when I was recovering from colon cancer surgery and trying to rebuild my income. Because of a weird confluence of events when I had changed jobs, I lost my health insurance. It was a simple oversight on my part, but a costly one, when I missed the sign-up for COBRA health coverage. During that lapse, I was diagnosed with colon cancer.

Suddenly I had to pay for all of my treatment out of pocket. My wife and I quickly burned through our savings and depleted everything else we had. We were unable to make payments on our house. I borrowed money from friends and family just to stay afloat.

The worst part was I couldn't seem to get my mojo back and make anything happen. I remember counting the change in the ashtray of my Audi 5000 just to see how much gas I could put in my car. Nothing was coming together for me. I responded to an ad in the newspaper for a sales position at Men's Wearhouse. I can vividly remember sitting down with the manager (who was probably ten years younger than me) in the back of the store at a small gray metal desk that looked like it came from an elementary school. This was *my* rock bottom. At that moment, I said to myself that I was better than this and resolved that it would never be like this again. From that day forward, it wasn't.

Looking back, I am thankful for that moment. Sitting in that room put the steel back in my spine, and it has never left. I vowed that it would never be like that again. My back was literally against the wall. At that moment, it was like a light bulb went off in my head. I decided to stop feeling sorry for myself, stop looking at want ads for a job, and start capitalizing on my relationships, my background, and my strengths. I looked for key influencers in my database and reached out to them. It took time and determination, but I was finally able to pull myself out of the hole. All it took was the decision to go to war and fight with everything I had.

Go to War

Sometimes when you face adversity and failure, you have to make a decision. For me it's like a switch is flipped in my brain and that's it. Game on. It's the same kind of process I went through when I was diagnosed with colon cancer at age forty. Back then, you weren't even supposed to start looking for it until you were fifty. Three days after my diagnosis, I was at the car wash, and I remember watching my car going through the assembly line, soap lathered all over it, and I just curled up, literally, on a bench. I remember just kind of lying on my side and thinking, *Is this how you're going to approach this, Bill? Curled up on a bench in a fetal position? Or are you going to go to war?*

In 1990, we didn't have the internet resources we have now, so information about colon cancer was limited. My sister worked for the American Cancer Information Service, so she sent me a bunch of brochures. I remember one said: "This is what you need to know about colon cancer." Armed with all the information we could find, we went on a mission to find the best doctors around LA. The first three opinions were dreadful. They all said that after surgery I would be incontinent, have sexual dysfunction, and have a colostomy bag… but that I would probably live. Not very promising.

However, the fourth opinion was different. That place had National Institutes of Health funding and had just started doing a new procedure that, if successful, meant I wouldn't have any of those complications. Because I had refused to give up and face failure, the fourth opinion completely changed my quality of life. It was that decision to go to war that kept me focused and rising up. That procedure is now routine, twenty years later.

Flip the Switch

There's a moment in time for all of us when we know with clarity what we have to do. Either we go to war and get better, or we curl up in the fetal position and wait for the end. A former client and friend, RJ Crosby, told me that when he is facing failure, his mantra is, "Adapt and overcome, reinvent yourself, and go for it." I believe you are the kind of person who straightens up, suits up, and goes to battle. You can say, "I can do better, and get better, because I have no other options and the alternative is unthinkable."

You may or may not have your back against the wall right now, but this might be your moment as you're reading this chapter to say, "I'm going to look in the mirror, recognize it for what it is, and recognize that I can do better, and commit to doing better now." You can choose to flip that switch.

My question to you is why wait? What if your back *isn't* up against the wall? Why not flip the switch now? It's a powerful realization when you discover that you don't have to hit rock bottom before you make a change that improves your situation. You can decide right now to evaluate and assess your situation and make a change that impacts your trajectory. Use this as that moment. Tom Ferry calls this an ABT culture. As previously noted, ABT stands for "always be testing." He told me, "People have this misconception that failure is a bad thing. But if you adopt this attitude of, 'Everything is a test until proven to be a repeatable and scalable part of my business,' then you're okay. If you adopt an ABT culture, *failure* is not even a negative word."

When you *flip the switch, start a war, and make things happen*, you change your trajectory and realize that failure doesn't have to be fatal.

Choose When to Fail

There's a mistaken idea that somehow failure happens *to* us and we are just like a ship helplessly tossed on a stormy sea. Sometimes the wave crashes over the boat and we capsize; other times it washes by and we survive. But this discounts our own complicity in our failures.

If I had paid attention to my COBRA insurance dates, I wouldn't have lost insurance coverage and become financially strapped with medical bills. Jocko Willink, author of *Extreme Ownership: How U.S. Navy SEALs Lead and Win*, calls this principle "extreme ownership." It means that we take responsibility for everything—even the things that we could easily blame on other people. This is especially true when it comes to failure. By taking ownership of your failure, you learn from it, hopefully before it ever happens.

Everyone has seen someone hit rock bottom. It's not a very pretty sight. Maybe you know someone with a drinking problem who got a DUI and then realized he or she needed to make a change. While hitting rock bottom may force you to change, wouldn't it be better to change before you have to?

Why wait until you hit rock bottom? Draw a line in the sand, plant a flag, and change now. There is always room for improvement, so decide now to improve. It may be your health, your disciplines, your sales strategy, your meaningful conversations with the people who matter most to you, or your attitude that you need to improve. Whatever it is that is pushing you toward the bottom, decide now to stop and change direction. Don't wait to fail; go ahead and confront it now *before* you hit bottom.

Let me pause for a moment to make something perfectly clear. I am not advocating that you fail, nor am I saying failure is inevitable. But at some point, things will not go as planned. Think ahead and anticipate what that might be so you can address it before it turns into a full-blown failure.

If you do everything possible and still fail, your attitude toward it will determine whether it is insurmountable or whether you can recover. Nick Palmisciano says:

> *I remember every failure that I have ever had and very few successes. That being said, I do not dwell on them. A failure only remains a failure if you quit. I try to learn as much as I can from every failure. Why didn't it work? What did I do wrong? Where could I have planned better? Then I move on, set a new goal, and keep pushing.*

Choosing *when* to fail helps you anticipate failure, so if it does happen, you'll know how to react and you'll spend the shortest amount of time reacting to it. Failing in practice helps you succeed in reality. In the military, there's a mantra that if you bleed in training, you'll survive in battle. You assess your mistakes, learn from them, and move forward. As Nick says, set a new goal and keep pushing. It's the only way to succeed.

Looking at the Dead Body

My wife, Toni, is a fan of crime shows. She enjoys digging through the clues along with the characters and trying to predict who did the crime. Shows like *Law & Order* or *NCIS* usually start with a dead body. The body is lying there in the crime scene with yellow "Police Line—Do Not Cross" tape strung up between signposts and trees and car mirrors. Around the body, the detectives murmur to themselves and one another and then one makes a witty comment before the screen fades to a commercial break. The rest of the show is spent re-creating the victim's moves, studying whom he or she knew, and revealing the choices that led to the person's untimely demise.

It may be a bit of a morbid example, but I use a similar exercise with my coaching clients. I have them think about the dead body—in this case their failure. I have them envision a scenario thirty, sixty, or ninety days in the future, in which they continue down the path they are on. Then I get them to tell me what it looks like. This exercise is powerful because it highlights areas where that future path may end in failure, but it also points out areas where it will end in success. It's like a morbid twist on Stephen Covey's "begin with the end in mind."

Creating a virtual view of failure can paint a vivid picture of the future. It's self-evaluation that helps you take a look at your life and decide if you should keep doing the things you've been doing. If you continue doing the things you're doing in your business and life, where will that take you? Spend some time visualizing that.

My friend and boss Daniel Harkavy, coauthor of *Living Forward: A Proven Plan to Stop Drifting and Get the Life You*

Want, advises readers to plan their funeral and write their eulogy now. If you died right now, what would that look like? Is the life you've created acceptable? The reader is then challenged to create "legacy statements." These are statements that solidify the person the reader wants to be at a point in the future, in the accounts (spouse, parent, financial, health, and so on) that are important. Thinking about how you want to be remembered helps you to be certain you are taking actions that lead to that vision.

How to Overcome a Failure

No matter how great your plan, how strict your discipline, how thorough your training, or how resolute you are in the face of fear, at some point in your life you will experience failure. It's inevitable. The best of the best choose to see failure as a gift for growth. They assess and evaluate it and make course corrections along the way. Failure, although painful, provides a deeper understanding of what we are made of and an opportunity to come back better and stronger and equipped to tackle the challenges ahead.

From the coach's chair, when a client has lost a sale or experienced a failure, I'll often describe the "NTSB investigation." When a plane crashes, members of the National Transportation Safety Board descend on the site and gather every piece of evidence they can find. They cart it back to the lab and begin the laborious process of putting the pieces together to try to find out what went wrong.

You need to do the same thing. If you want to overcome the failure and learn from it, you have to gather around the smoldering wreckage of the plane crash of your failure. You put on your NTSB windbreaker and pick up your clipboard and try to assemble the cause of "the crash" so that you can learn from it and eliminate the variables that caused it for next time.

The most difficult part of learning from failure is recognizing that whatever it is that happened, happened. It's over, and you can't go back and change it. It's important to disassociate from the emotion of the failure, step back, and look at it clinically to see what lessons there are to learn. What could you have done differently? Were there sequential issues that occurred? Did one wrong step put you off track and cause you to crash? If you can answer these questions and learn from those answers, then there's something you can change next time.

I see scenarios like this in the mortgage industry all the time, although the experience is universal to everyone in sales. A client will tell me he just lost a deal. A prospective customer was looking to buy an eight hundred thousand dollar house. The sales pro put a lot of time into it. He and the client had great rapport. Then the customer went dark. When he finally reconnected, he apologized, but he decided to go with another lender.

One of my clients tells me she's cut to the core when this happens: "I put all this time into it. People must understand that the only way I get paid is on commission." Of course, my clients are hurt and a little angry, because they feel like they wasted their time. But I coach them to analyze the situation. Keep the prospective client in the database and follow up. Don't slam the door on the person. Lean in a little bit and say, "I totally understand it. I wish you luck in that, and if you have any questions through the process, just let me know." Stay in touch—nurture the relationship for the long term. You may have lost this skirmish, but not the war.

After you have suffered a setback or a failure, this approach goes against everything you want to do. However, what I've seen is that there's always a good chance that something will fall through. Perhaps the deal that sounded too good to be true was too good to be true. Maybe someone will drop the ball. If you've taken a gracious position and stayed in touch, you might get the client back. Even if you don't, the odds are good that you'll get a referral down the road, because the person thinks so highly of you.

After that, assess: what could you have done differently? What are the lessons that you can learn from this? Is there a sign to watch for in these circumstances to prevent it from happening again? What system could you put in place for next time?

A crash-site analysis is never fun. You get to see the devastating wreckage of failure, but it is the only way to ensure that failure doesn't happen again.

Own What Went Wrong

In *Extreme Ownership*, Jocko Willink tells a story about a nightmare situation that occurred during the Battle of Ramadi in Iraq. While his SEAL team was out on a mission, they got into a firefight with a group of insurgents. When they realized that they were dangerously close to where another SEAL team was positioned, he discovered how close they had come to disaster:

> *Blue on blue—friendly fire, fratricide—the worst thing that could happen. To be killed or wounded by the enemy in battle was bad enough. But to be accidently killed or wounded by friendly fire because someone*

had screwed up was the most horrible fate.
It was also a reality.

In the days that followed, Jocko fretted over the consequences of this failure that had happened under his watch:

> *All the good things I had done and the solid*
> *reputation I had worked hard to establish in*
> *my career as a SEAL were now meaningless.*
> *Despite the many successful operations I had*
> *led, I was now the commander of a unit that*
> *had committed the SEAL mortal sin.*

The failure had occurred, and although thankfully no
lives were lost, Jocko and his team still had to make sure it
never happened again:

> *Frustrated, angry, and disappointed that*
> *this had happened, I began gathering*
> *information. As we debriefed, it was obvious*
> *there were some serious mistakes made by*
> *individuals during the planning phase and*
> *on the battlefield during execution. Despite*
> *all the failures of individuals, units, and*
> *leaders, and the myriad mistakes that had*
> *been made, there was only one person to*
> *blame for everything that had gone wrong*
> *on the operation: me.*
>
> *As the SEAL task unit commander, the*
> *senior leader on the ground in charge of the*
> *mission, I was responsible for everything in*
> *Task Unit Bruiser. I had to take complete*

ownership of what went wrong. That is what
a leader does—even if it means getting fired.

The goal of owning up to your mistakes is simple: to make sure they never happen again. When you look at what caused a failure, determine how you are responsible and identify ways to correct the problem. It doesn't eliminate the sting of failure, but it mitigates its effects.

Hold a Mission Debriefing

In the previous chapter, we talked about the importance of a well-defined plan to your mission's success. But a plan must continually be adjusted. It is refined through the fires of battle and becomes stronger for the next engagement. In the military, they hold a mission debriefing after each mission to determine what went right, what went wrong, where improvements can be made, and so on. It's called an "after-action review." It guides future missions by building on the successes and strengthening the failures of those of the past.

It is helpful to mimic this process after each "mission" that you tackle. Your missions could be as simple as a prospecting phone call to a new client or as complex as a new strategy to expand your market share. What is universal is that there is always room for improvement, but you won't know where to improve until you debrief.

Major Bob Hart recognizes that failure stinks, yet it offers the best opportunity for growth in the long run:

> *As a type A personality, [I have found that] failure sucks but also provides a great opportunity to learn and grow. I don't know of anyone who has never failed, and I'm not*

sure I want to follow a leader who doesn't know how to leverage failures to learn and become leaner, more efficient, more resilient, and better prepared. Learn from it when possible. Identify when and where things turned that led to failure, and don't make the same mistake twice.

We conduct an after-action review after most major events (training or combat operation) and dissect it down to the single actions—as professionals, we are always striving for perfection and to learn to do things better. Utilizing failure to motivate yourself to improve performance and prevent future mistakes is healthy and the key to both personal and institutional growth.

There is a difference between being smart and having wisdom. Wisdom is experience, and that often includes failure. I take failure personally and am often my own worst critic. If I fail, I feel as though I have let my guys down, and to me, personally, it is unacceptable. But I also try to learn from that failure to grow and become stronger and better prepared.

I Learned About Selling from That

Flying magazine always features an article called "I Learned About Flying from That." It is a true story of a flying situation and the lesson learned from it. For example, many years ago when I sold airplanes, an instructor hopped into a Bonanza to fly to Las Vegas. Halfway over the mountains between the San Fernando Valley and Las Vegas, the engine seized and he had to land the two hundred thousand dollar airplane in the desert. He had a lot of explaining to do. When he had done the preflight, he checked the oil but forgot to put the dipstick back in. As he flew, the engine pumped out all the oil. All of us were quick to learn from his very expensive mistake to always double-check the oil and the dipstick. You can bet we pushed that dipstick down and made sure it was locked in place every time after that. We did a mission debriefing, essentially, and learned from his mistake.

The same is true for sales. The Mission Debrief Guide is a simple one-page guide that helps you gather the details of your mission and determine what went wrong and what went right. (You can download a copy of the Mission Debrief Guide at WhiteCollarWarriorBook.com.) It begins with a one-sentence statement of a *mission goal*. Write what you wanted to accomplish here. (As a side note, if the mission failed, it may be that your goal was too broad to accomplish.)

Below the goal, write three to five lines that are a *mission summary*. Write this in such a way that you can highlight the main ideas of what happened. Your goal should be for a person who is unfamiliar with the mission to walk away with an understanding of how it went down. List both good and bad things here.

The next step is to fill in the *three buckets* (control/no control/influence). These three buckets provide a way to determine which things you can control and influence, and therefore improve, and which things you can neither control nor influence and therefore must let go. By reviewing your mission and filling these three buckets, you can clearly see where you can improve and where you will have to learn to maneuver differently.

The final two steps in the Mission Debrief Guide are *lessons learned* and *systems to implement.* You will need to be honest with yourself and your team about the lessons learned. It requires vulnerability to own up to all phases of a failure—especially if they weren't your fault or were outside of your control. These lessons can also be things that worked well, of which you should do more. Next to each lesson learned, try to determine a system or process you could implement that would lead to future success. For the good lessons learned, the system could be to train more team members to do that good thing. For the bad lessons learned, a system might prohibit that bad thing. The goal of the system is to streamline the process and set up future success.

The Mission Debrief Guide is an invaluable tool to help set you up for and sustain success even through the wreckage of failure. Denis Waitley has said, "Failure should be our teacher, not our undertaker. Failure is delay, not defeat. It is a temporary detour, not a dead end. Failure is something we can avoid only by saying nothing, doing nothing, and being nothing." Decide now to embrace your failures and learn to be better.

Check Plans, Change Accordingly

No matter how much you plan and prepare, things look different once your plan goes into action. Military warriors know this is true, and many of the greatest battles in modern warfare didn't play out like they had been drawn up. During the Allied landings at Normandy on D-Day, many of the bombs that were supposed to take out German defensive positions missed their mark. Soldiers landing on the beaches had to storm these strongholds under heavy machine gun fire. Paratroopers were dropped miles away from their landing zones and had to regroup to find the rest of their platoon behind enemy lines with much of their equipment lost during their jumps. Plans are great from the relative safety of the command center, but they often have to be adjusted when the battle rages.

I've discovered that part of the fear that paralyzes the sales professional comes from overplanning. Some of my coaching clients are great strategic thinkers. They are like chess masters who pride themselves on the ability to think several moves ahead of everyone else. That would be great if they were playing chess, but life is seldom like a chess match. It's fluid, it changes, and there are variables that manifest themselves only once you begin moving.

You are reading this book because you are a sales professional who wants to improve. Chances are you've developed instinctual reactions to the problems you've faced. The D-Day soldiers who ran into enemy fire didn't have to look to management to be told to lie down, cover fire, and move to safety. They saw the bullets flying their way, watched their comrades being gunned down, made split-second decisions, and began bravely fighting back.

When things don't go as you planned, don't give up or walk away. Use your brain, act instinctively, and make wise decisions. One of the greatest things about being a salesperson is that most of the responsibility falls to you. One of the worst things about being a salesperson is that most of the responsibility falls to you. Own it.

Embrace this reality. Take responsibility for your actions. Don't let fear of failure paralyze you. Check your plans, but then change accordingly. You'll learn something about yourself, and you'll give your customers a reason to trust you with their business in the future.

Closing the Failure Gap

No one sets out to fail—especially driven competitors striving to be the best in their field. But failure comes with the territory, and the best of the best learn from failure and use it to fuel future growth. There is a powerful video ad produced by Gatorade featuring some of sports' greatest stars. Michael Jordan, JJ Watt, Peyton and Eli Manning, Serena Williams, and Matt Ryan all share the secret to victory.

What's the secret? The tagline says it all: *Make Defeat Your Fuel.*

Failure will happen. In fact, the more ambitious your target is, the longer the fall if you don't make it. But the greatest use failure to push themselves onward and upward. They refuse to let one defeat define them. They keep moving, keep pushing, and keep striding. And if you do this too, in the end that failure may become your greatest gift for growth.

Assess

- Dealing with failure can be a learned response. Who influenced how you deal with failure? What positive or negative responses did you learn from this person?

_____

_____

_____

_____

_____

- Who is the "greatest" failure you know? In other words, who is someone you know who failed mightily but overcame that failure to become even better than before?

  _____

  _____

  _____

  _____

  _____

- What has been your greatest success? What did you learn from it?

  _____

  _____

  _____

  _____

  _____

- What has been your greatest failure? What did you learn from it?

  _____

  _____

  _____

  _____

  _____

Apply

- What lessons can this discussion around failure teach you? How can you apply these lessons to your own trials and struggles?

  _____

  _____

  _____

  _____

  _____

- Did you learn more from your greatest success or your greatest failure? Which lessons were more impactful in your life?

  _____

  _____

  _____

  _____

  _____

Maintain

- What is one area in your life where you need to take extreme ownership for mistakes? How would this shift in mindset help you to become a better person? How would it influence how others view you?

_____

_____

_____

_____

_____

Mission Debrief Guide

Mission goal (a one-sentence summary of your target):

_____

_____

Mission summary (three to five lines that summarize how the mission/target went down; include good and bad):

_____

_____

_____

_____

_____

THE 3 BUCKETS:

1. Things I can control (can be improved):

_____

_____

_____

_____

_____

2. Things I can influence (can be improved):

    _____

    _____

    _____

    _____

    _____

3. Things I can't control or influence (I have to let them go):

    _____

    _____

    _____

    _____

    _____

Lessons learned:

-
-
-
-
-

Systems to implement:

-
-
-
-
-

CHAPTER 8

MOTIVATION

Lesson 6: Your Motivation Matters Most When You Feel the Worst

"If you don't design your own life plan, chances are you'll fall into someone else's plan. And guess what they have planned for you? Not much."

—*Jim Rohn*

The movie *Blackhawk Down* is a dramatic account of the Battle of Mogadishu that occurred October 3–4, 1993, in Somalia. What was supposed to be a simple one-hour mission to send in members of elite Special Forces teams to snatch a high-profile target quickly turned into a two-day rescue operation. In the harrowing battle that ensued, the Special Forces were outnumbered and outgunned but fought valiantly.

There's a scene in the movie in which a commanding officer who is battle-weary is refitting for another trip into the battle zone. Another soldier asks him, surprised, "You're going back in?"

His simple response: "There's still men out there." In the rest of the exchange, the commander talks about motivation. He says that when he is stateside, people always ask him why he does it. Why does a soldier continue to put himself in harm's way time and again? Is it duty, honor, country? Is it the adrenaline rush or an addiction to danger? Is it competing with himself to be the best he can be? Many of those things come into play, but he says the reason he keeps doing it is simple: you do it for your brother standing next to you. It's as simple and complex as that.

I don't know if a conversation like this really happened on October 4, 1993, but it wouldn't surprise me. As I've interviewed warriors of all ages from all generations, this theme continues to rise to the surface. And it's always been that way. If you listen to World War II interviews in which soldiers tell of their time on the battlefield, they say the same thing. Is the sense of patriotism there? Absolutely. Are they doing it for God and country? Absolutely. Many of these soldiers have said that although they never wanted to go to war, they wouldn't trade the experience for anything, and their fundamental motivation is the person in the trenches next to them.

They don't want to let their brother down, so they do everything to survive, to keep pushing, and to stay motivated no matter what. Marcus Luttrell is depicted in the movie *Lone Survivor*. As he battled Taliban forces and watched his brothers die, he had one thought: a responsibility to survive to tell the story on behalf of his brothers. It was bigger than self-preservation. He was doing it for them.

The 2016 Atlanta Falcons football team embraced the concept of "in brotherhood" too. They had a truly magical season, setting records for their high-scoring offense and ultimately playing their way to the Super Bowl. Their brotherhood formed after an incident in 2015 when head coach Dan Quinn witnessed two players on the same position group asking for each other's phone numbers. Dan realized that although they were on the same team, they weren't "brothers." Dan reached out to an organization of former Navy SEALs, who went in and taught leadership and team building to the team. "In brotherhood" became the mantra of the 2016 Atlanta Falcons team, and ultimately it was the brotherhood that watched a twenty-eight-to-three lead over the New England Patriots disappear and lead to the most crushing defeat for the high-flying Falcons.

The Falcons turned the page on the heartbreaking end to the 2016 season and have vowed to keep pushing and striving for their brothers. Will they succeed? Time will tell, but the lessons they learned in defeat will push them to strive for greater victories. Their brothers are depending on it.

So how does this apply to you, a White Collar Warrior? Who are your brothers in the world of sales? Of course, no one wants to let his or her team or organization down, but is that really enough to get you to engage your motivation and push through the difficult times? Probably not. Every salesperson I've coached has gone through a funk. They've hit the wall, faced a difficult season in life, and let themselves and their team down. Sometimes this awareness makes it even worse.

But there's another group of "brothers" that you may refuse to let down—your family. I've seen it time and again with sales professionals. Families come in many shapes and sizes, and everyone's family looks different. But no one wants to let his or her family down. You may be married with a family of your own or single and just getting started in your career. No matter. Whomever you consider your family to be, they are your "brothers"—your core motivation. In the military, the safety of a brother is the motivation. For you, a salesperson, the well-being of your family is likely often what motivates you. An exercise I've used with some clients is to have a picture of their family on their desk, facing them, as a constant reminder of this simple truth and ultimate motivation.

The Power of Perseverance

As mentioned previously, one of the first steps in becoming a United States Navy SEAL is Basic Underwater Demolition and SEAL (BUD/S) training. It's not for the faint of heart. In fact, it's designed to push people to their very limit. BUD/S demonstrates the power of perseverance and the importance of motivation. Marcus Luttrell talks about not giving in to the pressure of the moment. He says that whenever you're hurting, just hang in there and finish the day. Then if you're still feeling bad, think about it long and hard before you quit. Perseverance means you take things one day at a time.

Marcus describes how some guys dropped out the week before the infamous Hell Week. These guys were just thinking ahead, dreading the forthcoming five days. They were anticipating the pain instead of dealing with it one day at a time. Perseverance and motivation start when you get your mind in the right place. When you decide, "I will not quit—no matter what!" Other SEALs have said they found success when they realized their instructors were not going to kill them. So what did they do? They worked down from death: "If they are not going to kill us, then I'm just going to get through this. I'm just going to put one foot in front of the other and focus on getting it done."

While perseverance in the sales environment pales in comparison to what has been described to me by the veterans I've interviewed, it is nonetheless critical in overcoming the obstacles that you will encounter. In sales those obstacles can include:

- Losing a deal
- Losing a referral relationship
- Encountering objections
- Dry spells

In the case of losing a deal or relationship, my best coaching advice is to bury that disappointment under a mountain of positive, "control what you can control" activity. It is fascinating to me that over the years, the salespeople who brought the "I lost a deal/relationship" stories into coaching sessions were always the ones who didn't have enough activity in their pipeline. Conversely, the White Collar Warrior with a full pipeline never even mentions those stories. Instead, a lost deal is chalked up to the cost of doing business. Ultimately, the momentary losses or downfalls are buried under a mountain of positive activity, which leads to the desired results—every time. Instead, our sessions are focused at the ten-, twenty-, or thirty-thousand-foot level—seldom on the runway.

Sales is a funny business. There is often freedom in your schedule, but that means you have to make wise choices about where and how you spend your time. It is all too easy to drift off into relaxing but unproductive activities, like scrolling through Facebook, checking in on ESPN, or any number of other things. The White Collar Warrior commits to the activities that predictably lead to results. He or she pushes through the temptation to wander and perseveres on the trek toward success. Remember, you have to earn the cigar before you celebrate, and you have to persevere to earn the cigar. Never give up on the disciplines that bring you closer to your goal. Dig deep and don't quit.

The Mastermind Effect

A large part of motivation is simply the company you keep. Jim Rohn famously said, "You are the average of the five people you spend the most time with." It's amazing how much your motivation can increase or decrease depending on whom you hang out with. Don't get me wrong; I believe motivation comes from within, and I'll address it later in the chapter, but whom you are around can increase or decrease your motivation.

It all starts with what you put in your mind. I call this the voices in your head. It's simple: what you put in comes back out later. If you fill your mind with the right words, the right thoughts, and the right influences, they will come out later when you need them most. On the other hand, when you fill your mind with negativity, self-doubt, and discouragement, those too will come out. But they'll come out when they will do the most harm.

I get to coach a lot of top producers in their individual industries, and I've discovered some similarities among them. They start out as highly motivated individuals, but they have a strong circle of friends who keep them motivated and moving in the right direction. I call it the "mastermind effect." When top producers are around other top producers, they talk differently, they think differently, and they move differently. They high-five one another, they celebrate, they challenge, they trash talk—they're very much like the military. They are a team, and although they may work for different organizations or are in different departments, they still have the same goal. You'll see that same kind of reaction in the military. Even though there is competition between units and branches, they all fight for the same goal.

The flip side of that is seen in something called the "crab theory." Crabs in a bucket will climb over one another to reach the top. But when they get to the top, an interesting thing happens. The crabs on the bottom start to pull down the crabs that are closest to the top. Those crabs once on top slip and slide back down to the bottom, and the whole futile cycle begins again.

There's a study in which a group of monkeys was put into an enclosure. In the center of the enclosure was a pole, and at the top of the pole was a group of bananas. As the monkeys climbed the pole to reach the bananas, they were shot with a blast of cold water. Every time a new monkey would almost reach the bananas, it would be drenched with a blast of icy water. As you can imagine, eventually they gave up, and the bananas were left untouched. In the second part of the experiment, they replaced all but one of the monkeys that had been drenched with new monkeys. As the new monkeys tried to climb the pole to reach the bananas, the monkey who had been hit with the icy blast dragged them down. This happened over and over, so the new monkeys never even got a chance to reach the top.

I've seen this with clients I've coached. If you are surrounded by people who either don't want you to succeed or have tried and failed themselves, they can become a negative pull on you. They will try to drag you down if you climb too high, or they will discourage you from even trying based on a negative experience they've had.

The Mastermind Effect works, but it's up to you to surround yourself with positive people—people who will likely extend you a hand because they've gone where you want to go. If you don't have access to these people, listen to podcasts or read books in order to put the right messages into your brain. The effect on your motivation will astonish you, and you'll find the courage to dig deeper and go farther than you thought you could.

The Impact of Culture

Another interesting and related effect on motivation is the impact of culture. Culture can play a huge role in the motivation of individuals. People do what people see. I had a client once who had just joined a company. When he took the call with his soon-to-be boss offering him the job, they hammered out a start date for the following week. He asked his boss what time he needed to be there that day and threw out the time of 8:00 a.m. On the first day of the new job, he got to the parking lot at 7:45 a.m. Since he didn't have keys to the building, he waited for his new boss. Around 8:20 a.m., the boss rolled in. The next day the same thing happened. After about a week, my client realized that he could begin work at 8:20 every morning if he wanted, because his boss had set the tone.

This happens all the time. People show up later, they stretch their lunches a little longer, and they criticize the top producers, creating a culture of disincentives. Whether you are a leader in your organization or a member of the rank and file, it's important to realize your impact on the company's culture. If your actions and your words are negative, you could be demotivating the people around you and unknowingly damaging the entire organization.

Ironically, I've seen organizational cultures demotivate the very sales team they depend on. One killer move is to ignore the salesperson. And it's not uncommon for sales managers to close their door and put out brush fires all day but not be available or encouraging. The lack of interaction with their teams fails to engender trust. Because they don't know what to do or haven't been trained well themselves, they sequester themselves and fail to connect with their teams.

Good culture has the completely opposite effect. It brings out the best in people and forges a team that is all-in together and motivates the team. Twenty years ago when I was in the hospital with colon cancer, we told the nursing staff we didn't want any negative conversations in there; we were just going to talk about positive things. I wasn't denying the reality, but my attitude was, "I'm gonna heal, and I'm gonna get out of here." We placed motivational quotes on the walls in the room. My wife made chocolate chip cookies and kept them in there, because it created a positive environment. The nurses wanted to come by and visit. The result was that I healed quickly. In fact, I healed so quickly and did so well that the surgeon used to have newly diagnosed people call me for support and encouragement for the next ten years. He wanted me to tell my story because it gave other patients the motivation to fight and to survive.

When I work with successful sales leaders, I see that they create a positive culture. They listen, encourage, and remind people of their why and motivate them to succeed. It's a small thing, but the results are huge.

Motivation Is Intrinsic

Here's a secret about motivation: the best motivation—*lasting* motivation—is intrinsic, not extrinsic. Think about it: there's no shortage of platitudes everywhere to encourage you. You can find motivational quotes on social media, T-shirts with catchy slogans, signs to hang on your walls, and bumper stickers to put on your car. They all sound good, but they won't motivate the unmotivated.

Why does it take a heart attack to get someone motivated to eat healthier, exercise, and lose weight? Why must a person lose his or her family to finally quit drinking? Did no one who cared try to motivate these people? In most cases, people have friends or family who try to motivate them to stop bad behavior, but people will only really change when they flip the switch on the inside. Why? Because motivation is intrinsic. You can change only when you want to change.

When I dive into motivation with coaching clients, we start with finding their why. I ask them point-blank: "Why are you doing this?" More often than not, I get general platitudes. "I want to make more money." "I want to be successful." "I want to prove something to others and myself." These all may be true, but they aren't enough to motivate you to push past difficulties and thrive.

Knowing your why is the first key to moving forward. It equips you to push through the pain and keep going when you just want to quit.

3 Components of Intrinsic Motivation

Daniel Pink, in his book *Drive: The Surprising Truth About What Motivates Us* offers the following:

1) Mastery: "How Do I Become Better?"

I'm in my early sixties and am continually trying to get better. Every day, you're either growing or stagnant. The choice is up to you. I'm always looking for ways to get better, to master my craft. Is there a book that I can read? Is there an event that I should attend? Is there a person whom I should talk to who can make me a better coach? Mastery motivates me to be the best I can be at what I do. It lights a fire that burns from the inside out. How can you continually get better at sales to become a sales master?

2) Autonomy: "How Can I Exercise My Own Judgment?"

Autonomy allows you to exercise your own judgment and decide what you need to be working on and when. The autonomy that I have as an author and a coach working with Building Champions motivates me to make things happen on my own. I know what needs to happen, so I make the best choices I can. Autonomy makes me feel like I'm making my own decisions and choices for my own business. The more I feel like it's my own business, the more motivated I am to make it succeed, because I know it's up to me.

3) Purpose: "Am I Driven to Keep Pushing?"

Mastery and autonomy both move me toward a driving purpose in my world. As a coach, I want to feel like I'm pouring white paint. That's my analogy. I'm hungry for new ideas, solutions, and technologies, and I'm pouring white paint into my world, to my tribe that follows me. I'm encouraging them, inspiring them, and providing examples that will help them to see what's possible, to remind them of the things that they're no longer doing, to share with them things that they could do that they haven't done before. That's what drives me to keep pushing every day.

Calibrate Your Day

The simple truth is that motivation will ebb and flow. The harder the task, the more you have to dig deep to keep pushing. The military elite don't always feel top notch, but they suck it up and do their jobs. Darren Hardy, in his training program called Insane Productivity, refers to "calibrating your day." I love this thought.

To calibrate something means to dial it in and fine-tune it for optimum use. You'll never be motivated if you feel off. Calibrating your day means you start from a place of success. Find some activator that reminds you why you are doing what you are doing. It may be looking over your business vision or life plan. It may be a sticky note on your bathroom mirror or a picture of the person you want to become. It may be reading over your By Noon Effect plan and making sure you're on track. It may be choosing a podcast to listen to on the way to work or reading a section of a book.

Calibrate your day around something positive, and it will feed you. When you calibrate your day, you are feeding your mind with truth that will come out at just the right moment. When that vision is freshly in your mind, it reminds you who you are becoming. It sets you up for success so that when you have a choice about which path to take during the day, you will choose the person you want to be, not the person you were. When you have that vision, you are calibrated. You move toward who you want to be. You lean in and embrace the process.

Pack Your "Go Bag"

In the military, when they deploy, they take what's called a "go bag." A go bag has everything a servicemember needs so they can go at a moment's notice. They need very little time to prepare. They just grab it and go. When they are on a mission, it is even more streamlined. They call it a chest pack, and it has velcro loops where they can stick extra magazines, first-aid kits, flashlights, tourniquets, and anything else they might need. They are truly ready for action. If you want to keep your motivation high, you need to have your professional go bag packed and ready. You can fill it with the right input. Maybe it's training that prepares you to become the person you want to be. If you are a person of faith, maybe you have Scripture that motivates you. You might have a Zig Ziglar or Jim Rohn quote or story that inspires you. You could have a book by Tony Robbins or others. Whatever you do—resist news. Nothing good is going to come from putting news in your go bag.

Filling up your go bag keeps you engaged. Your bag contains the weapons and resources you need to be ready to fight the inevitable wall that you will sometimes hit. When you hit resistance, you will need something to help you push through. Filling your go bag with the necessary tools keeps you moving forward and ready for whatever comes your way.

Focus on Your Why

Once you've calibrated your day and packed your go bag, there is one more step that is critical for moving forward with motivation: remember your why. Your why is the reason you do what you do. It's that intrinsic motivation that burns deep down inside like a fire. It keeps you moving no matter what the obstacle and how deep the resistance. Without it, you'll cave under pressure and snooze through opportunity.

The major thrust of the book *Living Forward* is to create a life plan. This is just what it sounds like. It's a plan for your life. As a Building Champions coach, I have walked hundreds of clients through the life-planning process. It's very in-depth, but at the end of the process, clients have a plan that dramatically increases the odds that they will get where they want to go rather than drift someplace else.

A life plan invariably will connect some dots between business and life. What do you think about when your feet hit the floor in the morning? Why do you do what you do? Chances are, if you are already crystal clear on your life plan and business vision, your motivation is solid too. If things are still fuzzy, these two tools can help you clarify your purpose and make sure it connects with your actions.

If you want to keep your motivation high, you need to do some form of a life plan. It doesn't have to be super in-depth, but it should outline some goals and hopes and dreams for your life. It should have specific and measurable checkpoints that keep you on track. It should review last year and ask some questions like: What has gone well this year? What hasn't gone well this year? Which relationships do you feel best about? What are some of the things you have the most regrets about? Most important, where do you want to end up? (To access and download the life plan and business vision plan, go to WhiteCollarWarriorBook.com.)

The second tool that will keep your motivation high is the business vision plan. A lot of people get confused about this. They feel like they have a business plan that guides their business, so why do they need a business vision? The difference is small but important. A business vision is designed to get you thinking about what you want your business to look like a year, two years, three years out. A life plan could be twenty, thirty, or forty years out. The business vision is shorter term. You want to try to view it with what Daniel Harkavy calls "bifocal vision." This means you can look down at the present while simultaneously looking out at the future.

So you have to ask: What does my business look like today? Who are the clients I'm doing business with? What is my average commission? What fills my days? What activities am I involved with? What are the things I don't want to be doing two or three years from now? What are the things that I want to delegate?

Answering these questions will allow you to create your "vision future." Your vision future is a description of a day in your future life. It might look something like this:

> *I park my Jaguar in the spot with my name on it. I walk into my corner office, and I spend a few minutes looking at my 100-gallon saltwater fish tank. I sit down at my spotless desk, and I look at my calendar for the day. I have two appointments. I notice on my calendar that it's date night tonight with my wife; this is something that I never used to do. And I think, "Life is good."*

I want you to picture the image you have of your own success. Remember the "look at the dead body" concept from the last chapter? This is the antithesis of that. This move paints a picture of what your business and your life could look like if you are motivated to make it better.

> *"People don't buy what you do; they buy why you do it. And what you do simply proves what you believe." —Simon Sinek*

Closing the Motivation Gap

Remember the three B's: belong, become, and build. What do you want to belong to? What are you becoming? And what do you want to build? The answer is found in your convictions—in your why. We all want to belong to something bigger than ourselves. For you it may be a part of a particular team or a level of success in your industry. We should all work on becoming something more than we are now.

Do you know what you want to become? Remember, if you are sitting still, you are becoming stagnant. Look to your convictions and allow them to guide your steps.

Finally, what do you want to build? This is your legacy. It's much easier to stay motivated through the setbacks when you know they are pushing you farther toward your goal. When you know why you do what you do, motivation comes naturally. It's fuel for both the good days and the bad days. It drives you on in spite of the resistance. And it equips you to fight for yourself and those you care about most.

Assess

- Think about a time when you struggled to keep going. What motivated you to continue?

_____

_____

_____

_____

_____

- Who is one person you would absolutely hate to let down? How could you use that to motivate yourself through the tough times?

  _____

  _____

  _____

  _____

  _____

- I made the case that motivation is primarily intrinsic. Do you agree with this statement? Has external motivation or internal motivation been more impactful in your life and career?

  _____

  _____

  _____

  _____

  _____

- Have you ever worked in an organization where the culture demotivated you? How did you overcome it?

  _____

  _____

  _____

_____

_____

Apply

- Schedule a day to craft your life plan and business vision. (Date: _____) How can having a clear picture of the future you want help you push through your struggles today?

_____

_____

_____

_____

_____

Maintain

- Who is the most positive motivator in your corner? Who is the most negative? What could you do to add more positive motivation to your life?

_____

_____

_____

_____

_____

- Could you articulate your why in a simple sentence? How can you use that to motivate you when things get tough?

  _____

  _____

  _____

  _____

  _____

CHAPTER 9

TEAM

Lesson 7: Your Growth Depends on Your Team

*"There is no such thing as a self-made man.
You will reach your goals only
with the help of others."*

—*George Shinn*

You have to take ownership for your success if you want to be the best. Until now in our journey together, the focus has been inward on the steps you can take to ensure your success. We've talked about the importance of your training to lay the foundation of everything you do. Our military elite friends showed us the power of discipline as key to determining your success. We faced fear and turned it into your friend, then discovered the critical role that planning plays in your future success. We learned how failure can paralyze and how it can actually become a catalyst for growth. Most recently, we reconnected with your motivation and discussed how you can still push forward regardless of how you feel.

Each of these chapters involves something *you* can do to become a warrior. But in this chapter, we'll look at what is possible once you begin to consistently practice the Way of the Warrior and learn the key to your most explosive growth—surrounding yourself with a team.

The right team is an unstoppable catalyst for growth. The wrong team can bring it to a screeching halt. So the first question is how can you build the right team if you don't already have one in place? You may be a solo operator—or think you are. How do you go from one to two, from two to three, and so forth? And if you already lead a team, whether as a sales entrepreneur or as a sales leader as part of a larger organization, how can you maximize the effectiveness of your team? As you read this chapter, consider which of these questions applies best to your situation, but don't skip over any parts. Whether you've been functioning as a "Lone Ranger" to this point or working on a team, you can learn valuable lessons to take your growth to the next level and become a White Collar Warrior.

A Catalyst for Growth

Think for a moment about some of the tasks during your workweek that you absolutely crush. They're in your sweet spot. You can almost do them with your eyes closed. You likely do those things extremely well—better, in fact, than most. You might even say you are or could be among the elite at doing those things. Now think about the things you hate doing. They slow you down and feel like drudgery. When you do them, it feels more like you are slowly slogging through the sales swamp. Doing those things takes you away from the tasks you enjoy and generally leaves you feeling drained.

Now, we all have things that we have to do that we don't enjoy. That's just a fact of life. But what if someone else with different strengths and skill sets actually enjoyed doing those things you despise? What if that person could happily do the things you don't like to do in order to free you up to do what you do best? Oh, and better than you. How cool would that be? (Can you feel the hope surging inside you already?) Such is the beauty of a team.

The fact is we all are hardwired in a certain way to do and enjoy certain things more than others. Some people like being front and center. They thrive in the spotlight. Others prefer to be backstage and derive joy from seeing operations run smoothly. Some people love the thrill of chasing leads and closing sales. They're good at it. Other people love to manage a process, run an office, and keep the books. They're good at it. Knowing how you are wired helps you work best on a team.

You must be candid in your assessment of your strengths and weaknesses. No one can do it all, not even the elite. It's critical that you be honest with yourself and your team about where you operate the best. In the military, only a handful serve as snipers, rangers, SEALs, or fighter pilots, but without a strong support team, they simply couldn't do much. When a fighter pilot takes off from an aircraft carrier, hundreds of people had a hand in preparing for mission success. When a SEAL team is inserted into hostile territory, it doesn't go alone. An entire support team—from logistics to drone operators, transportation to technology—assists. Without that team, the elite SEALs' talents would be lost.

If even the elite need a team surrounding them to perform at their best, so do you. A well-designed team fulfills three objectives:

1. **Maximizes strengths**. When individual team members are empowered to do what they do best, the entire team shines. As the saying goes, "A rising tide lifts all boats." When the individuals of a team thrive, the entire team thrives.

2. **Minimizes weaknesses**. Just as every member has strengths, every member has weaknesses. That's why we all have blind spots. A good team knows the weaknesses of its members and has a plan to "team" around them. Team members do this primarily by complementing weaknesses with other members' strengths.

3. **Multiplies impact**. Good team members sharpen one another. They forge bonds through triumphs and tragedies. They have a shared history. They compete in a friendly way to bring out the best in one another. Just as one person can lift only a finite amount of weight, one person working alone has a limited capacity. A good team pulls together the best of its team members and increases the capacity of the team as a whole.

> *"SEALs…fight in teams, only in teams, each man relying entirely on the others to do exactly the right thing. That's how we do it, fighting as one in a team of four or maybe even 10 or even 20, but always as one unit, one mind, one strategy. We are, instinctively, always backing up, always covering, always moving to plug the gap or pave the way. That's what makes us great."*

> —*Marcus Luttrell, Lone Survivor*

The only reason the Special Forces elite are free to focus on doing what they do remarkably well is because they are part of a well-designed team, not only in their smaller cohort but also beyond. It's why they're often called the leading edge of the spear. When you implement this same type of thinking in your own sales career, you can deploy your natural strengths to achieve your very best results.

It is so common for me to see in coaching that clients spend little time doing the two or three things that generate the most results, because they are bogged down in the minutia of the business—things they should not be doing. Focusing on the few things that generate the most lift is a common theme in coaching.

Start Small

You generally ease into developing a team, but where it starts is with the recognition that you've plateaued; you feel tapped out, like there just isn't any more time in the day. When you reach the point where you don't see how you can grow by working harder, you need to expand your influence through a team.

Let me offer a quick word of caution here: don't be a martyr. It may feel good (for a while) to do it all yourself and bask in the glow of your hard-earned self-made successes. But that's a one-way ticket to burnout. Then you'll lose all the momentum you worked so hard to build. Simply put, that strategy is not sustainable.

At this point you may be saying, "Wow! I get it! But how am I going do that? I'm already doing all I can." Good news: you can and should start small.

Start by discovering what it is you would need your team to do. When I coach clients who want to develop a team, we start with a proven exercise I call "Delegate Down." Start by taking a snapshot of what you actually do during the day. Get a journal and record what you do all day, every day, in fifteen-minute increments. We refer to this as "time tracking." It's like being an attorney, accountable for billable hours for a week, but it's worth it. Yes, it can feel tedious, but until you know exactly where your time is going—cold, hard data— you won't know where you most need help. After a week of this time tracking, the results will be eye-opening.

Once you have that data, organize all your tasks into three buckets:

- **HPAs**—high-payoff activities. A high-payoff activity is an income-producing activity. It may be giving a presentation to a prospect where you can close and secure a sale. Obviously, you want a lot of HPAs on your calendar.
- **MPAs**—medium-payoff activities. A medium-payoff activity might be organizing your day and determining whom you want to connect with and what exactly you will do to keep the pipeline full. This activity may not earn you income today or tomorrow, but it is critical for long-term success.
- **LPAs**—low-payoff activities. A low-payoff activity would be something like submitting expenses, addressing envelopes for handwritten notes, or preparing a sales report. These are things that need to be done, but they don't need to be done by you.

When you start seeing your day through this paradigm, you can more easily identify the LPAs and where a team could improve your effectiveness.

The best way to start small but still retain a measure of control is to hire a virtual assistant. Gone are the days when you need to add permanent staff to start building a team. You may be able to pay someone a little extra to work through your database, address some envelopes, or tackle the administrative tasks that bog you down. If you're part of a team in a larger sales organization already, you may have access to more help than you realize. Over the years, I've heard countless executives complain that their sales teams simply don't use all the resources made available to them. So get creative. There may be a receptionist willing to help out. If you work in a more restrictive corporate environment, maybe you don't have the luxury of just hiring somebody. But what if you tried to think outside the box a little bit? Is there another way to do it? Are there assets in the corporation that you're just not utilizing? As Thomas Edison said, "There's always a better way....Find it!"

Bottom line: if you've been pounding your head against the wall thinking you have to do this alone, you need to understand something. The elite warriors in the military don't go it alone—why should the elite in the sales world? Change the way you're thinking. There are always ways to make the most of what you have; sometimes it just takes a little creative thinking to come up with a solution.

Sometimes my coaching clients push back on this suggestion to get an assistant. After all, it may seem self-important to hire an assistant. *Just who do you think you are?* One of my fellow Building Champions coaches, Jerry Baker, puts it like this: "Capacity precedes production." Steve Smothermon in his book *Big Problems, Bigger God* puts it this way: "You have to prepare for growth before you can have growth." If it feels strange to hire a professional assistant, try this out. Do you have (or know) a teenager you could hire? Could you pay that person to take some of the LPAs off your plate so you could focus more on HPAs? It's mutually beneficial. You'd be giving someone an opportunity to earn some money for a task that is tedious for you. What would an extra hour or two or three be worth to you? How much could you earn as a result of investing a little of someone else's time each week?

That sort of thinking is the beginning of thinking in terms of *team*. You need to crawl before you can walk, and you have to start somewhere. By tracking your time through the Delegate Down process, you'll identify your LPAs and prepare to delegate them. If someone else can do something at least 80 percent as effectively as you, let that person do it.

Growing Pains

Starting to build a team can be as simple as hiring someone to take the LPAs off your plate so you can focus more on HPAs. But managing a team has challenges, especially if you've been operating in "Lone Ranger" mode for a long time. It's important to have systems in place to help you navigate the challenges and bring out the best in your team and you.

Two simple steps will help dramatically. First, *over*communicate. Second, be abundantly clear about expectations. The biggest breakdown in teams occurs when there is a miscommunication or no communication. If you've been taking care of business on your own for a while, it can be easy to work through problems and details in your head. When you add team members, however, it's important to remember that they don't know what's going on inside your head. They need to hear you say what you are thinking and what you expect from them.

Clarity brings unity and focus. It starts with the job description, but before you can write a job description, you need to have clarity yourself about what you need. I see a lot of busy salespeople make this mistake when they need to hire somebody. In the mortgage world, for example, a sales pro might need someone to package a loan to prepare to submit it to processing. So in a burst of energy, the busy pro hires a person—anyone who's breathing—forgetting the maxim "Hire slow, fire fast." Hiring the wrong person quickly can cause more problems than not hiring at all. Being slow to hire, I always tell clients, means being very clear about the job description and what the expectations are of the candidate up front, to ensure the role is a good fit for both my client and the prospective team member. A great way to begin is to describe the behavioral traits of the ideal candidate first. I'll often have clients do this with me in a session. I'll capture the words they use to describe the ideal candidate, and then I email them to the client. The pro tip is to then use those descriptors in a social media post with a "Who Do You Know?" or "Our Team is Growing" headline. It's uncanny how many great candidates this brings to the surface for clients, and it has the bonus of telling the rest of your tribe that you are busy and growing—a good thing!

After you hire the right people, meet with them daily at first, then weekly as they settle into the role. You cannot overcommunicate at this stage! People will naturally gravitate toward the things they enjoy most, whether those things are the priority or not, so it's important for you to keep in front of them what *you* determine to be most important. Keep them focused on the correct tasks and going in the right direction, and don't let them go off into the weeds. A little extra maintenance at this stage of growth will go a long way toward sustainable success. I don't mean you should micromanage people, but train them to do what they need to do to free you up to do what you need to do. The old training maxim is critical at this stage: 1) *tell* them what you want them to do, 2) *show* them how to do it, and 3) *watch* them do it and then praise or redirect.

The Gatekeeper Effect

When it comes to being abundantly clear in training, consider Michael Maher. Michael is a Realtor in Atlanta who wrote a fantastic book called *The Seven Levels of Communication: Go From Relationships to Referrals*. I've interviewed him several times, and I always walk away with new insights. He has done a terrific job of equipping his team to do what he does not have to do without alienating clients.

When you call Michael's office, you don't get Michael; you get his assistant, who has been trained to answer professionally: "Michael Maher's office. How can I help you?" When you say, "I was referred to Michael Maher. I'd like to talk to him about selling our home," she replies, "Yes, sir. That's what I do here at Mr. Maher's office. How can I help you?" She takes ownership of the situation. You don't get through directly to Michael. You start with the gatekeeper.

This Gatekeeper Effect didn't just happen. Michael had to prepare his assistant to help callers understand that this is how the onboarding system works. This process is a familiar one. When you call a surgeon, she doesn't pick up while in the middle of an operation. You start with the physician's assistant—the gatekeeper who works closely with the expert—in your case, *you.*

Michael's assistant may then say, "I know Michael would want to know a little bit more about your situation before you talk. Would you mind if I ask you a few questions to help make the most of your time?" Michael has equipped his team to understand the importance of the initial contact and not have the client feel brushed off or stonewalled. When you think about developing your team, it is critical to set expectations and script those initial interactions—not just for the team but also for your clients and customers.

When you focus on identifying the proper tasks, meet with team members frequently to make sure that they're on task, and establish a process for them to correctly do their jobs, you create an environment where the entire team flourishes. Don't make assumptions about the people you're bringing on board. Overcommunicate and be abundantly clear, and you'll solve 90 percent of the problems before they ever occur.

Connecting to Your Team

Some of you may already have a team in place. If so, to maximize your own growth, you must maximize the growth of your team. Daniel Harkavy developed a unique Team Assessment Tool that we use at Building Champions. It gives a wonderful starting place if you want to take your team to the next level. (To access and download the Team Assessment Tool, go to WhiteCollarWarriorBook.com.)

This invaluable tool helps empower a sales team leader to bring out the best in the team. Using the Team Assessment Tool enables you to dig deep into the eight key areas. As you can see, this tool lets you go much deeper than a simple tactical overview of the job requirements.

1. Industry strength
2. Greatest strengths
3. Greatest area to improve
4. Fears or obstacles
5. Greatest area to focus on
6. Coachability
7. Work-life balance
8. Number-one expressed need

The number one expressed need is a game-changer. It builds communication and accountability into your team. I've used it when coaching organizations and heard responses like: "I need to be encouraged. Words of affirmation are important to me. The more you tell me I rock if I'm doing well, that'll fuel me to be even better" and "I could do a little better with work-life balance. I know I'm staying too late. I'm probably working too much." As a leader, you can then say, "Fair enough. Let's work on that."

Another key component this assessment uncovers is coachability. It answers the question, "Are you willing to be sharpened?" Daniel has a great line he uses to open the improvement conversation with team members: "Can I coach you on this?" Very few people will say no when you ask for permission first. Coachability starts when you spend time with people. Having a regular dialogue and conversation is critical to understanding who your team members are as individuals. It is also vital to seeing who you are, and can become, as a leader.

Closing the Team Gap

No matter if you are an individual sales pro who needs to build a team or you need to maximize the team you already have, the Team Assessment Tool is a vital starting place. If you're building a team, begin looking at the eight buckets to determine what type of team members to add in order to multiply your strengths and manage your weaknesses. If you are a team leader, use this tool to connect with your team members and guide them to be their best.

Whether or not you currently have a team, the time-tracking exercise is a must to discover how and where you spend your time. Doing this helps you discover your HPAs, MPAs, and LPAs so you can make better decisions about where to invest your time. You'll likely discover opportunities to delegate down. Start small. Access resources you may have overlooked or get creative and hire a virtual assistant or someone you know. Look for time-draining, repetitive tasks that need to get done, just not by you, and give them to someone else to manage. Keep that person accountable and focused by scheduling a daily meeting, and then transition to a weekly meeting to keep that person on task.

As a sales leader, a lot of times you don't know what you don't know. It's easy to think everything is a numbers game in sales, but people are not numbers. Don't give in to the thought that getting the right people is essentially a numbers game. Embrace the mantra of the military: "Leave no man behind."

If you embrace the philosophy of no one left behind, you will be more intentional about how you select, hire, and train your team. Your perspective will change. You'll focus on finding people you want in the trenches with you every day. You'll choose teachable people with whom you can build win-win relationships. You'll focus on "brotherhood," camaraderie, and closeness. Sure, some people won't work out. Attrition will happen. But this is your elite unit! Raise your sights and develop a team that pushes you to grow to your fullest potential.

ASSESS

- In terms of a team, where are you now? Do you have a team to help you grow, do you manage a sales team already, or do you need a team to help you go to the next level?

  _____

  _____

  _____

  _____

  _____

- What are your key strengths? How do you use them to your advantage? How might you use them to develop a team?

  _____

  _____

  _____

  _____

  _____

- What are your primary weaknesses? How do you overcome them now? Whom could you add to your team to shore up these weaknesses?

  _____

  _____

  _____

  _____

  _____

APPLY

- How might you access the underutilized resources around you and put them to work for your benefit? What's stopping you?

  _____

  _____

  _____

  _____

  _____

- Invest a week or two in tracking how you spend your time in fifteen-minute increments throughout the day. Journal your results, and at the end of the week evaluate them. What stands out to you?

  _____

  _____

_____

_____

_____

Maintain

- Identify your HPAs, MPAs, and LPAs from the results of your time-tracking. Make a list of the things that you need to delegate immediately to focus on higher-payoff activities.

_____

_____

_____

_____

_____

- Find someone to take those LPAs off your plate so you can be free to focus on what matters most. Who would that be? What are the next steps?

_____

_____

_____

_____

_____

CHAPTER 10

THE REWARD OF THE WHITE COLLAR WARRIOR

"I have been impressed with the urgency of doing. Knowing is not enough; we must apply. Being willing is not enough; we must do."

—*Leonardo da Vinci*

There's a well-known scene in the movie *Braveheart* in which William Wallace, portrayed by Mel Gibson, rides his warhorse up and down the line in front of a ragtag bunch of Scottish warriors who make up the Scottish rebels. As this band of warriors lines up on the hill, they can look across and see the much-better-equipped English army. They have better armor, superior weapons, a cavalry, and a plan. The Scots are terrified, and rightly so.

At this point, William Wallace has made a name for himself. He's the fierce individual who stood up to the English nobility, and he's made it his mission to fight for freedom for Scotland. He's a fearsome sight, with blue war paint streaking his face and a five-foot-long broadsword sheathed diagonally across his back. As he runs up and down the line of warriors, he utters these words:

> *Sons of Scotland, I am William Wallace, and I see a whole army of my countrymen here in defiance of tyranny. You've come to fight as free men, and free men you are. What will you do without freedom? Will you fight? Fight and you may die. Run and you'll live, at least a while. And dying in your beds many years from now, would you be willing to trade all the days from this day to that, for one chance, just one chance, to come back here and tell our enemies, "They may take our lives, but they'll never take our freedom"?*

If you've seen the movie, you know what happens next. William goes to pick a fight with the leaders of the English army, and the Battle of Stirling ensues. William's rallying cry unifies the Scots, and they engage in the bloody battle for freedom.

A Call to Arms

I'm not wearing blue war paint on my face, and I don't have a broadsword on my back (though I do have a replica of that sword hanging in my office) to help you slay your enemies. But I do want to issue a rallying cry for you, White Collar Warrior. Today is your day, and you must make a choice. Do you want to stay where you are, content with the status quo? Or do you want to use the lessons in this book, gleaned from over twenty years of coaching high performers and borne out on the battlefield with the military elite, to radically change the way you do business?

The choice is yours, and ultimately you will live with the decision. Changing the way you do things is never easy, but it is vital if you want to grow. You can become the warrior who takes charge of your life, accesses every weapon and tool at your disposal, and fights the enemy head on. Sometimes that enemy is you.

I've given you the blueprint for success. The seven lessons that make up the Way of the Warrior are here in black and white. I've given you the tools and the framework to make incremental changes to your day, your week, your month, and your year that will equip you to stop drifting through life and start going where you want to go.

Let's recap the seven key lessons:

Lesson 1: Your Training Is the Foundation for Everything

When legendary football coach Vince Lombardi would begin football training camp for the Green Bay Packers late in the summer, he would start with the basics. He would pick up a football and begin with the most elemental statement of all: "Gentlemen, this is a football." Coach John Wooden began his UCLA basketball training camps in much the same way—he taught his players how to tie their shoelaces and put on their uniforms.

Training often feels redundant. It's repetitive. It often covers something you know how to do and therefore take for granted. It's an obstacle you want to quickly overcome so you can put what you've learned into action. But military warriors and sales warriors know that constant training is vital to success. It drills deep into your core and creates habitual pathways that kick in when you are in the thick of battle.

Training makes you physically tough by making you mentally tough first. It instills in you an unwillingness to waver, a dogged determination to never give up, and a plan to master in private what you will display in public. Training is the foundation for everything.

Lesson 2: Your Discipline Will Determine Your Success

According to Jocko Willink, discipline equals freedom. If you are a sales professional, you were likely drawn to sales because of the freedom it can provide. In many ways, you act as your own boss. You have the autonomy to make decisions that impact your bottom line. How hard you hustle determines how much money you bring home. But you have to earn the cigar before you celebrate.

Developing a disciplined routine keeps you on track and helps you discover that freedom you seek. For the military elite, maintaining discipline when things go sideways is a matter of life or death. As a White Collar Warrior, lack of discipline can lead to death by a thousand cuts. You may not bleed out all at once, but if you lack discipline, the effects can snowball and the consequences can become dire.

Discipline keeps you accountable and ensures you pay the price for your success. Without it, you will not succeed. With it, you will establish core practices that equip you to reach your goal.

Lesson 3: Your Fear Must Become Your Friend

It's been said that everything you want is on the other side of fear. Yet fear has a way of blinding you and paralyzing you so that you don't act. However, fear can be a powerful motivator if you harness it and put it to work. In fact, fear can actually become your friend.

The quickest way to overcome fear is to tackle it head on. The best way to do that is to be honest with yourself about the worst-case scenario. Often, this is way worse in your head than anything that could ever happen. And even if the worst case did happen, by thinking about it ahead of time, you start to establish a path forward. Once you've considered the worst-case scenario, you can then use your fear to maximize your production. Start by shifting your mindset. In sales, often your biggest fear is fear of rejection. Every no gets you closer to a yes. Shift your mindset and you'll deflect your fear. Then establish a process that harnesses all the best parts that are uniquely you.

Fear must become your friend if you hope to become a White Collar Warrior. There is power when you face it head on and use it to further your growth. Put that power to work for you, and your fears will diminish.

Lesson 4: Your Sales Plan Positions You for Mission Success

No plan is ever perfect. But just because there are no perfect plans doesn't mean that you shouldn't plan. A sales plan is vital for mission success. Without it, you have nothing to aim for. Without a clearly defined plan, it is impossible to measure success.

The best and brightest in the military make plans based on the readiness of their forces; the tools, people, and equipment at their disposal; the intel about the enemy; and the proximity of their objective. As a sales warrior, you must do the same thing. Take stock of what you have and what you don't. Take note of your position in the marketplace and that of your competitors. Make a plan to leverage your strengths and shore up your weaknesses. Combine them all and make the best plan you possibly can. Launch, then improve. Great leaders improvise and adjust. The right plan positions you for mission success; how you adapt takes you the rest of the way.

Lesson 5: Your Failure Can Be a Gift for Growth

Failure is painful. It wounds your pride, it's embarrassing, and it can be miserable to experience. Yet it can also be a wonderful gift for growth. Failure is rarely final or fatal. The only way a failure is truly a failure is if you are unable or unwilling to learn from it.

Every failure you experience pushes you closer to success. When football players get tackled, they can either fall backward or push forward. Failing forward is the way to grow. Look at your life up to this point and consider the ways you've failed. They probably spring easily to mind. What lessons did you learn from these failures? If you don't know, then you need to spend some time reflecting and evaluating. Capture these lessons and use them to grow and move forward.

Lesson 6: Your Motivation Matters the Most When You Feel the Worst

Zig Ziglar once said, "People often say that motivation doesn't last. Well, neither does bathing; that's why we recommend it daily." When you are motivated, you feel like you are on top of the world. There is no task too big to conquer, no challenge you can't tackle, and no hill you won't climb. The world is at your fingertips, and it's yours for the taking.

But when motivation wanes, that's when it matters most. If you are even tempted to "ring the bell," you are done. But by surrounding yourself with others who keep you strong, you build a culture of motivation that enables you to achieve more and push through those down times. The military elite have a strong brotherhood. They know that if they give up, they would let their brother down. This stubborn grit and determination empower them and get them through the tough times. Motivation matters most when you feel it least.

Lesson 7: Your Growth Depends on Your Team

Whether you already lead a team or are a solo operator in need of a team, one thing is true: no one gets by for long alone. The poet John Donne said, "No man is an island entirely of itself." If you want to take your growth to the next level, you have to access the power of a team. Military warriors do not operate alone. Every member is part of the larger system. As members fulfill their individual functions, they multiply their individual effectiveness.

The right team around you can become a catalyst for your growth. The right team helps bring out your strengths and hone them to a razor's edge. Similarly, a well-designed team helps balance the weaknesses that are often your blind spots. The best teams help you focus on your high-payoff activities while delegating lower-payoff activities to a team member who's better suited for the task.

You will always reach a point where you just can't do any more on your own. At this point, a team becomes vital for scalability and growth. Learn this lesson now, and your future growth will be assured.

You Can Do This

In the first chapter, I described Scott, a White Collar Warrior from St. Louis, who started the day with this mantra: "Do what most will not do, to enjoy what most never will." I want to encourage you one more time. You can do this. I've seen the results from countless others just like you. They started with a desire, bought in to the process, and reaped the results. But it took doing what most would not do to enjoy what most never will.

It will take training, but everything you want in life is uphill. So climb that hill and train like never before. Practice in private so you can perform in public. It will take discipline. You'll have to get up earlier than you want to, make calls that you'd rather not make, trust in the process when it seems to be going nowhere, and play the long game when the quick win beckons. But discipline will keep you focused and on track. It will require you to face your fears head on and stare them down. You'll have to imagine the worst to experience the best.

Along the way, you'll realize that fear can become your friend when you allow it to empower you. You'll have to develop a firm yet flexible sales plan to get where you want to go. This plan will have all that you know and all that you've learned and will focus it on the mission at hand. It will take failure as you try things that you think will work, only to discover a flaw in your thinking. No matter. Pick yourself up. Dust yourself off and do it again. Learn from your mistakes and use them to strengthen your resolve going forward. It will take digging deep to find the motivation that you didn't know you had. You'll stare down disappointment and discouragement as you stiffen your spine, grit your teeth, and charge forward. When you feel the worst, your motivation matters the most. Finally, it will take a team of people in your corner who have your back. They will tell you the truth to make you better. They'll create opportunities for your strength to shine. They'll rally together around a common mission. They'll fill in the gaps where you have weaknesses. They'll create margin for you to do the few things that generate the greatest results—the things that only you can do.

And together you'll summit the peak and experience success. You can do this.

You have what it takes to succeed. You have the tools at your disposal. You have the lessons that other White Collar Warriors have passed on. You have the principles that military warriors have fought, bled, and died to protect. You have a swim buddy to help you, push you, and drive you on. Together we'll close the gap between where you are and where you want to be.

I believe in you. Let's go. Your future awaits.

ABOUT THE AUTHORS

 A strong supporter of the U.S. military, **Bill Hart** has been on the front lines of sales and business for more than twenty-seven years. He currently lives near Los Angeles, CA, and coaches business professionals and executives as part of Building Champions.

Bill Blankschaen is an experienced collaborative writer, content creator, platform strategist, and the author of several books, including *A Story Worth Telling: Your Field Guide to Living an Authentic Life* and multiple collaborative books. He is the Founder and Chief Story Architect of StoryBuilders and Content Director for the *Secrets of Closing the Sale Master Class* with Kevin Harrington and Zig Ziglar.

ENDNOTES

1 Marcus Luttrell and Patrick Robinson, *Lone Survivor: The Eyewitness Account of Operation Redwing* (New York: Little, Brown and Company, 2013).

2 Mark Divine, interview by Bill Hart, January 2014.

3 Luttrell and Robinson, *Lone Survivor*.

4 Sean Parnell, interview by Bill Hart, January 2014.

5 Andrew Paul, interview by Bill Hart, January 2014.

6 Patrick Lencioni, *The Ideal Team Player: How to Recognize and Cultivate the Three Essential Virtues* (Hoboken: Jossey-Bass, a Wiley Brand, 2016).

7 Mike Wooley, interview by Bill Hart, January 2014.

8 Wooley, interview.

9 Bob Hart, interview by Bill Hart, January 2014.

10 Nick Palmisciano, interview by Bill Hart, January 2014.

11 Tom Ferry, interview by Bill Hart, January 2014.

12 Robert Pirsig, *Zen and the Art of Motorcycle Maintenance: An Inquiry into Values* (New York: HarperTorch, 2006).

13 Hart, interview.

14 Luttrell and Robinson, *Lone Survivor*, 140.

15 Paul, interview.

16 Parnell, interview.

17 Ferry, interview.

18 Holly Reed, interview by Bill Hart, January 2014.

19 Palmisciano, interview.

20 Hart, interview.
21 David Allen, *Getting Things Done: The Art of Stress-Free Productivity* (New York: Penguin Group, 2001).
22 Gary Keller, *The One Thing: The Surprisingly Simple Truth Behind Extraordinary Results* (Austin: Bard Press, 2013).
23 Charles Duhigg, *The Power of Habit: Why We Do What We Do in Life and Business* (New York: Random House, 2014).
24 Hart, interview.
25 Nick Palmisciano, interview, January 2014.
26 William McRaven, commencement speech, University of Texas at Austin, May 17, 2014.
27 Max Leaman, interview, January 2014.
28 Leif Babin and Jocko Willink, *Extreme Ownership*: *How U.S. Navy SEALs Lead and Win* (New York: St. Martin's Press, 2015).
29 Ferry, interview.
30 Reed, interview.
31 Tim Ferriss, *The 4-Hour Workweek: Escape 9-5, Live Anywhere, and Join the New Rich* (New York: Harmony Books, 2012).
32 Larry Kendall, *Ninja Selling: Subtle Skills. Big Results.* (Austin: Greenleaf Book Group Press, 2017).
33 Duhigg, *The Power of Habit*.
34 Reed, interview.
35 Wooley, interview.
36 Chad Fleming, interview by Bill Hart, January 2014.
37 Ibid.
38 Luttrell and Robinson, *Lone Survivor*.
39 George W. Dudley and Shannon L. Goodson, *The Psychology of Sales Call Reluctance: Earning What You're*

Worth in Sales (Dallas: Behavioral Sciences Research Press, 2008).

40 Steven Pressfield, *The War of Art: Winning the Inner Creative Battle* (New York: Black Irish Entertainment, 2002).

41 Ibid.

42 Hart, interview.

43 Reed, interview.

44 Palmisciano, interview.

45 Ferry, interview.

46 John C. Maxwell, *Failing Forward: Turning Mistakes into Stepping Stones for Success* (Nashville: Thomas Nelson Publishers, 2000).

47 Palmisciano, interview.

48 Palmisciano, interview.

49 Hart, interview.

50 Ferry, interview.

51 Ibid.

52 McRaven, interview.

53 Richard J. Machowicz, interview by Bill Hart, January 2014.

54 David Allen, *Getting Things Done: The Art of Stress-Free Productivity* (New York: Penguin Group, 2001).

55 Hart, interview.

56 David Berke, interview by Bill Hart, January 2014.

57 Ibid.

58 RJ Crosby, interview by Bill Hart, January 2014.

59 Ferry, interview.

60 Palmisciano, interview.

61 Harkavy and Hyatt, *Living Forward.*

62 Babin and Willink, *Extreme Ownership.*

63 Ibid.

64 Ibid.

65 Hart, interview.

66 Andrea Kremer, "Falcons aim to forget Super Bowl loss with Navy SEAL approach," *Sidelines* (blog), NFL.com, September 14, 2017 (12:17 p.m.), http://www.nfl.com/news/story/0ap3000000844656/article/falcons-aim-to-forget-super-bowl-loss-with-navy-seal-approach.

67 Marcus Luttrell, interview by Bill Hart, January 2014.

68 Steve Smothermon, *Big Problems, Bigger God: Whatever You Need for Whatever You Face* (Eugene: Harvest House Publishers, 2015).